The U.S.–Mexican Border Environment

U.S.–Mexican Border Communities in the NAFTA Era

Edited by Norris C. Clement

San Diego State University Press

Published by
San Diego State University Press
5500 Campanile Drive
San Diego, CA 92182-4403
http://www-rohan.sdsu.edu/dept/press

in collaboration with
Herberger Center for Design Excellence
College of Architecture and Environmental Design
Arizona State University
PO Box 871905
Tempe, AZ 85287-1905
http://www.asu.edu/caed/herberger/herbergerHome.html

This work is a study carried out by
The Network of Border Economics/Red de la Economía Fronteriza
(NOBE/REF)

Printed in the United States of America

ISBN-0-925613-35-5

The U.S.–Mexican Border Environment

U.S.–Mexican Border Communities in the NAFTA Era

SCERP Monograph Series, no. 4

A series edited by Paul Ganster, K. David Pijawka, and Anthony Brazel

---

Contributors

PRINCIPAL AUTHORS

NORRIS C. CLEMENT	SAN DIEGO STATE UNIVERSITY
SERGIO REY	SAN DIEGO STATE UNIVERSITY
GERALD L. SCHMAEDICK	NORTHERN ARIZONA UNIVERSITY
NOÉ ARÓN FUENTES	EL COLEGIO DE LA FRONTERA NORTE
ALEJANDRO BRUGUÉS	EL COLEGIO DE LA FRONTERA NORTE

SUPPORTING AUTHORS

J. MICHAEL PATRICK	TEXAS A&M INTERNATIONAL UNIVERSITY
LUCINDA VARGAS	FEDERAL RESERVE BANK OF DALLAS, EL PASO BRANCH
PAUL GANSTER	SAN DIEGO STATE UNIVERSITY
ANGÉLICA VILLEGAS	SAN DIEGO STATE UNIVERSITY

The Southwest Center for Environmental Research and Policy (SCERP) is a consortium of U.S. and Mexican universities dedicated to addressing environmental issues of the U.S.–Mexican border region through applied research, outreach, and regional capacity building.

SCERP Universities
Arizona State University
Colegio de la Frontera Norte
Instituto Tecnológico de Ciudad Juárez
Instituto Tecnológico y de Estudios Superiores de Monterrey
New Mexico State University
San Diego State University
Universidad Autónoma de Baja California
Universidad Autónoma de Ciudad Juárez
University of Texas at El Paso
University of Utah

SCERP website: www.scerp.org

Contents

Foreword

U.S.–Mexican Border Communities in the NAFTA Era is the final report carried out by the Network of Border Economics/La Red de la Economía Fronteriza (NOBE/REF), a network of researchers from universities and public institutions in the U.S.–Mexican border region. The study was supported in part by SCERP and the initial results of the effort were presented at Border Institute II in April 2000 and appear in the third volume of the SCERP Monograph Series, *The U.S.–Mexican Border Environment: Economy and Environment for a Sustainable Border Region: Now and in 2020*, in the chapter by Norris C. Clement and Sergio Rey, "The U.S.–Mexican Border Economy in the NAFTA Era: Implications for the Environment."

We are pleased to publish the present volume in the SCERP monograph series. SCERP's central mission addresses the environmental problems of the U.S.–Mexican border region and the consortium clearly understands the fundamental linkage between economy and environment in this region. Improvement of environmental quality and support of sustainable development practices are possible only with a strong economic base.

U.S.–Mexican Border Communities in the NAFTA Era is an assessment of the impact of NAFTA in the border region that uses a consistent methodology to better understand the economies and other features of the major Mexican and U.S. border communities. The study analyzes how the demographic, economic, infrastructure, and environmental characteristics of the border region have changed from the period prior to the North American Free Trade Agreement to 2000, six years after the implementation of the treaty. The findings of the economic analysis were juxtaposed with qualitative data from interviews with stakeholders from border communities in Mexico and the United States. The stakeholders included decision and policy makers from the public and private sectors as well as researchers and community representatives.

The perceptions of border stakeholders regarding the state of the environment under NAFTA presented a mixed picture. Most U.S. and Mexican respondents considered NAFTA's impact as a positive one in regard to issues such as focusing national attention on border environmental problems and improving cross-border cooperation on environmental problems. Yet, despite the environmental components of NAFTA, including the creation of the Commission for Environmental Cooperation (CEC), the North American Development Bank (NADB), and the Border Environment Cooperation Commission (BECC), along with the implementation of the Border XXI Program for the border environment, some two-thirds of the individuals in U.S. border communities interviewed indicated that the actual quality of the environment remained the same or worsened during the 1994–1999 period. Stakeholders in Mexican border cities were somewhat more positive, with about sixty percent of respondents reporting that the environmental quality remained the same or worsened in their communities. So, most U.S. and Mexican respondents saw no improvement in border environmental conditions, notwithstanding the significant federal effort in this regard. And, indeed, some noted a negative trend.

In a related question, both Mexican and U.S. border stakeholders ranked analytical tools for monitoring the environment last in priority, with demographic and economic modeling tools viewed as most important. The implication is that while most respondents perceive that environmental quality is not improving, they did not hold the environment as a high priority at the time of the survey research. Instead, local interest in the border was more attentive to the topics of demographic growth and the performance of the economy.

The editors of the SCERP Monograph Series hope that the present volume will help border stakeholders better integrate environmental themes with economic analysis. We, and our colleagues in SCERP and in border communities, are convinced that the quality of life along the border can be improved, but only through sustainable economic activities. We feel that *U.S.–Mexican Border Communities in the NAFTA Era* is an important step in understanding the interplay of environment and economy in the border region.

Paul Ganster, San Diego State University
K. David Pijawka, Arizona State University
Anthony Brazel, Arizona State University

SCERP Monograph Series General Editors

Acknowledgements

In addition to the principal and the supporting authors, the following individuals contributed immeasurably to the surveys and to the production of this volume: Catherine J. Happersett from the Social Science Research Laboratory at San Diego State University (SDSU); John Renison, SDSU, Imperial Valley Campus; Vera Pavlakovich, University of Arizona (Tucson); Thomas M. Fullerton, University of Texas (El Paso); José Alberto Rodríguez, El Colegio de la Frontera Norte, COLEF (Tijuana); Gustavo Banda, COLEF (Tijuana); Raúl González, COLEF (Tijuana); Alfonso Cortez, COLEF (Mexicali); Martin Herrero, COLEF (Nogales); Juan Parra, COLEF (Piedras Negras); César Mario Fuentes, COLEF (Ciudad Juárez); Cuauhtémoc Calderón, Universidad Autónoma de Ciudad Juárez (Ciudad Juárez); Julio César Morales, Universidad Autónoma de Ciudad Juárez (Ciudad Juárez); Eduardo Alarcón, COLEF (Nuevo Laredo); Belem Vázquez, COLEF (Matamoros).

I

Introduction

Background

The North American Free Trade Agreement (NAFTA) of the United States, Mexico, and Canada was implemented on January 1, 1994. Since then, trade and investment in the region have expanded dramatically and new NAFTA–related institutions such as the North American Development Bank (NADB) and the Border Environment Cooperation Commission (BECC) have been put into place. Meanwhile, NAFTA has been loudly praised by its proponents and mercilessly damned by its critics. The volume of books and articles analyzing its impact has steadily increased and efforts are underway to extend the agreement to the rest of the Western Hemisphere (Clement et al. 1999; Economic Policy Institute 2001).

Nevertheless, very little has been written about the effects of NAFTA on the highly urbanized communities of the U.S.–Mexican border region, which constitute the main points of contact between these greatly contrasting countries. In 1993, when ratification of the agreement was being debated in those two countries, most border communities were led to believe that NAFTA would bring them higher levels of prosperity, improved infrastructure, a cleaner environment, and better cross-border relations with their neighbors on the other side.

In 1999, five years after the agreement's implementation, this study was initiated in order to assess the validity of these expectations and to fill a gap in the literature on the impact of NAFTA. Most systematic studies have focused on NAFTA's impact at the national level, while most of the information available on U.S.–Mexican border communities has been anecdotal, published in relatively obscure academic journals, or scattered about in local newspapers.

NAFTA, of course, is only one of many factors that have impacted these communities in the period since the implementation of the agreement. Other factors, such as financial crises in Asia and Russia increased financial instability in most of the world's emerging economies and added to Mexico's economic woes during the latter part of the decade. Yet, perhaps the most important event during this period was the Mexican peso crisis of December 1994, which dramatically changed the dollar-peso relationship, turning Mexico's trade deficit into a surplus, and plunging the nation's economy into a deep, but relatively short, recession. This crisis resulted in a significant decline in retail sales in many U.S. border communities. The retail sector is of fundamental importance in most U.S. border communities and, in some cases, Mexican sales account for more than 50% of the total sales and 25% of the jobs in the community. Retail sales tax rebates are also an important source of funds for local governments. Additionally, a devalued peso means that many U.S. border residents find it worthwhile to make more of their purchases in Mexico, potentially further reducing retail sales and sales tax rebates on the U.S. side.

While the Mexican national economy was in crisis, lower wage rates in dollar terms and new regulations established by NAFTA made foreign investment generally more attractive in Mexican industry and specifically increased the appeal of the maquiladora (or assembly) industry. This resulted in an economic boom and near zero unemployment rates in the Mexican border region, despite high rates of internal migration from the interior of the country to the northern border region.

Ironically, at the same time that the Mexican economy was in crisis, the U.S. economy was enjoying one of the longest and strongest expansions in its history and a sustained stock market boom. Given the strong link between the health of the U.S. economy and the macroeconomic performance of the Mexican economy, the U.S. expansion clearly boosted Mexican exports, the Mexican national economy, and the local economies of U.S. border communities. Many of the benefits and costs of the economic expansion spilled over to the Mexican side of the border region. Meanwhile, democratic reforms and administrative decentralization (devolution of powers) in Mexico opened up new opportunities and challenges for subnational governments and gave border government entities increased flexibility for collaborating with their counterparts in the United States.

Organization of the Study

While it is possible to identify the main factors operating on these communities in the 1990s, no systematic analysis has been carried out to determine just how these widely differing border communities have fared during the NAFTA era, which roughly coincides with the decade of the 1990s.[1] This study attempts to remedy this deficiency in two ways: (1) through an analysis of existing demographic and economic data and (2) through a survey of knowledgeable persons from government, business, nongovernmental organizations, and academia in the main U.S. and Mexican border communities.

The study was carried out by members of a newly formed consortium of individuals and organizations in the United States and Mexico—the Network of Border Economics/Red de la Economía Fronteriza (NOBE/REF). This organization is supported by the El Paso Branch of the Federal Reserve Bank, which maintains a website (http://www.nobe-ref.org) and provides a point of contact for the consortium. San Diego State University (SDSU) and El Colegio de la Frontera Norte (COLEF) in Baja California also support NOBE/REF. Beyond the Federal Reserve Bank of Dallas, SDSU, and COLEF, NOBE/REF members include border-based universities and businesses, as well as Banco de México (Mexico's central bank) and Mexico's Instituto Nacional de Estadística, Geografía e Informática (INEGI), (National Institute of Statistics, Geography, and Information).

Objectives and Assumptions of the Study

This study, which focuses on the county-municipal level, has two main objectives:

1. To determine how the demographic, economic, environmental, and infrastructure situations in U.S. and Mexican border communities have changed during the NAFTA era.
2. To determine what kinds of demographic, economic, and quality-of-life indicators[2] and analytical tools are needed by these

communities in order to enable them to monitor and analyze their own situations on an ongoing basis.

The study is also intended to:

- Assist local, state, and national decision makers in both Mexico and the United States to better understand the complex situation of border communities and thereby develop more informed policies.
- Assist academics and other researchers to identify issues and trends that deserve further study as well as to develop the skills and contacts that will be required as NOBE/REF begins to implement its agenda of collaborative, border-related research projects.
- Assist the private sector, especially businesses and organizations located in the border region, by providing a more comprehensive analysis of the economies of the border and by updating the key indicators that businesses need to make decisions related to day-to-day operations and long-term investments and strategies.

A major assumption of the study is that, given the significant differences among the border communities, the impact of NAFTA and of other factors, such as the 1994 peso devaluation, have been and will continue to be different in each U.S. and Mexican border community. Despite these differences, however, it is likely that there will be some trends that are common, in varying degrees, to all border communities.

II

U.S.–Mexican Border Communities: An Overview

Geographically, the U.S.–Mexican border region is not well defined. In theory, it should be delineated according to the specific phenomenon being studied, such as environmental issues or cross-border commuter workers. However, in practice, the region is usually demarcated by the administrative units contiguous with the international boundary—that is, U.S. counties and Mexican municipalities (See Map 1). According to this definition, 25 U.S. counties and 38 Mexican municipalities form the border region. In 2000, this region had a population of 11.8 million (6.3 million on the U.S. side and 5.5 on the Mexican

Map 1: U.S. Counties and Mexican Municipios

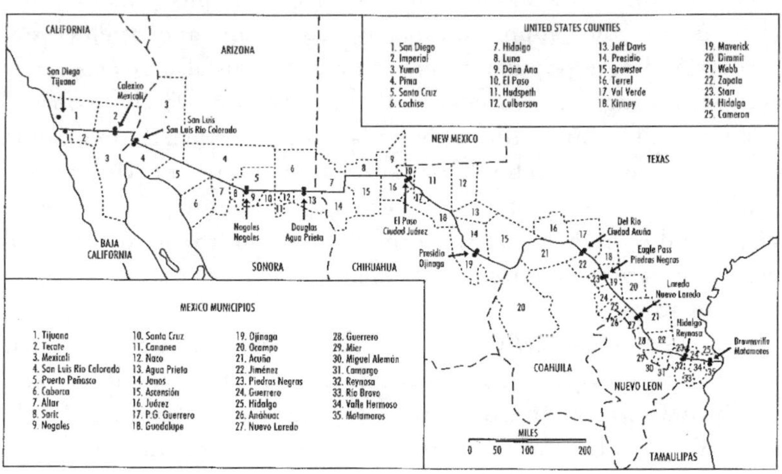

side), up from 10.6 million in 1995 (5.8 million on the U.S. side and 4.8 million on the Mexican side). Recent projections estimate that this population will reach somewhere between 15.0 million to 24.4 million by the year 2020, with a figure over 20 million most likely (Peach and Williams 2000).

In this section, an overview of the economic development of the U.S.–Mexican border region since the demarcation of the international boundary in the nineteenth century is provided. The next section gives a brief economic and demographic profile of each border community included in the survey. These sections are designed to provide an historical and geographical context for the data presented in subsequent components of this report.

The Economic Dynamics of the U.S.–Mexican Border Region

Complementarity and interdependence have characterized the border region since the initial demarcation of the international boundary between Mexico and the United States in the mid-nineteenth century. It is complementary because some products (goods and services) that are available on one side of the border are not usually available on the other, and prices vary significantly on the two sides. These conditions make the region interdependent through the creation of cross-border trade and investment. Further, the complementarity of the region's labor markets arises from "pull" factors in the north (labor demand created by higher wages and unfilled jobs) and "push" factors in the south (excess labor supply created by a stagnant and often unstable economy and high population growth rates). This also creates interdependence through cross-border market interaction, which, historically, has rendered the international boundary a porous membrane. Similarly, higher levels of technological development in the United States stimulate Mexican consumers and firms to buy those products that are cheaper and of higher quality on the U.S. side of the border while differences in natural resource endowments and wages draw U.S. tourists and firms to Mexico.

Thus, complementarity and interdependence, as two interrelated characteristics, have created structural cross-border links and a unique distribution of economic activity along the border. Historically, these links have provided the basis for rapid economic growth in the region.

Unfortunately, these same links have also made each side vulnerable to the economic fluctuations and deteriorating environmental conditions of the other side of the boundary. Still, during the 150-year period from the mid-nineteenth century through the beginning of the twenty-first century, the U.S.–Mexican border has become one of the most dynamic and integrated binational regions in the world.

The international boundary between the two countries came into existence after the Mexican-American War with the signing of the Treaty of Guadalupe Hidalgo (1848) and the Gadsden Purchase (negotiated in 1853). Over the next half century, the region's development was accelerated by the construction of an extensive railroad network, particularly in the 1880s, and large irrigation projects in the early 1900s in areas such as California's Imperial Valley. These public work projects stimulated the growth of the traditional sectors of mining, ranching, and agriculture. During this period, workers from the interior of Mexico and other countries were attracted to the border region by the rapid growth of jobs that, in turn, stimulated local cross-border trade, resulting in the development of U.S.–Mexican twin city pairs. Meanwhile, as trade between the two countries grew, the dynamic U.S. economy expanded westward, creating jobs and economic opportunities throughout the entire region.

For much of this time, the border was not a significant barrier to immigration and cross-border trade, and residents freely crossed the border to shop or work. The existence of a free trade zone (*zona libre*) in Mexico's border region during this period provided an incentive for Mexican citizens to populate the northern region and also stimulated commerce with the United States. The Mexican Revolution of 1910–1917 also contributed to northward migration as thousands of Mexicans fled the violence and property destruction of the war. However, smugglers, rustlers, robbers, and other people of questionable merit from both the United States and Mexico were drawn to the border region as well and contributed to the strife and lawlessness of the area. This created a high level of conflict between the two nations that lasted well into the twentieth century.[3]

In the 1920s, the prohibition of the sale and manufacture of alcoholic beverages in the United States contributed to the growth of new economic activities in Mexican border cities, especially in Tijuana and Ciudad Juárez. U.S. citizens, eager to find liquor and other forms of recreation, including gambling, flocked to Mexican border towns, stimulating a new kind of tourism. The end of Prohibition in 1933 and the beginning of the Great Depression restrained these activities in the 1930s, while the growth of military installations in the southwestern United States during World War II contributed to the continued economic and demographic growth in the region through the 1940s.

After World War II, a new phenomenon breathed fresh life into the border region—Sunbelt Migration. In addition to the continued growth of military expenditures in the region, U.S. corporations began to move into the Southwest in order to take advantage of new market opportunities. A gradual shift of the U.S. population from east to west and the growth of a low wage, unorganized labor force in the Southeast and the West made certain types of manufacturing—first apparel and then electronics—more attractive. In response to the migration of capital, more workers came to the region. In addition, the warm, sun-drenched winters attracted tourists and retirees from the Snow Belt of Canada and the northern United States.

Population expansion on the northern side of the international boundary also stimulated the growth of urban centers. Over time, this growth spawned retail stores and eventually large shopping malls that were used by U.S. residents and, increasingly, by Mexicans who regularly crossed the border as part of their customary shopping pattern.

Several factors led to this dramatic rise of cross-border retail trade.[4] Until the late 1980s, tariffs on imported consumer goods in Mexico were quite high—averaging about 40%, but reaching up to 100% for some items—and most Mexicans preferred imported, U.S. manufactured products to domestic ones. Additionally, between 1954 and 1976 the dollar value of the Mexican peso was held constant—12.5 pesos to one U.S. dollar—despite the fact that inflation in Mexico was significantly higher than in the United States.[5] This led to an overvalued peso, meaning that Mexicans could do better by converting their pesos into dollars and buying consumer goods in the United States rather than shopping in Mexico. Border residents and tourists from the interior of Mexico were allowed to bring in products up to a certain value for personal use. If they exceeded that limit, a tip or bribe (*propina* or *mordida*) to the customs inspector would usually facilitate duty free importation.

Cross-border trade gave rise to the growth of large retail sectors in most U.S. communities immediately adjacent to the international boundary and the associated jobs, incomes, and tax revenues came to play an important role in the economic development of those communities. Thus, during good times in Mexico, U.S. border communities tended to prosper, but when crises and devaluations of the peso occurred in Mexico, the U.S. communities would suffer as well.

The rise of cross-border trade in the post–World War II period did not escape the notice of Mexican authorities. In the mid-1960s, the Mexican government introduced the Programa Nacional Fronterizo or PRONAF (National Border Program) to counter the growing preference of Mexican border shoppers for U.S. goods. The two objectives of the program were to make the Mexican side of the border more attractive to U.S. and other foreign tourists and shoppers, and to make more Mexican national products available to their own residents. While the program had some success, cross-border trade still flourished, at least until the 1976 peso devaluation that changed the peso-dollar relationship from 12.5:1 to approximately 20:1. As a result, Mexican consumers, whose real incomes (adjusted for inflation), as well as dollar-equivalent incomes declined, found it cheaper to shop in Mexico, causing U.S. border retailers' revenues to shrink dramatically. Subsequent devaluations in the period 1982–1994 brought frequent and wide fluctuations in cross-border commerce.

Another key element in the economic dynamics of the border is the maquiladora (assembly) industry. This sector grew indirectly out of the termination of the Bracero Program (1942–1964), a guest worker program designed to supply temporary Mexican workers to alleviate U.S. farm labor shortages. The Bracero Program brought in millions of workers during its 22-year existence but was subject to a great deal of controversy. Not only were workers sometimes exploited, but the program did not eliminate undocumented migration into the United States. It did kindle strong demand for Mexican workers that still exists today and has expanded into many sectors of the U.S. economy in most regions of the United States.

Upon termination of the Bracero Program in 1964, Mexicans who lost their jobs in the United States flooded back into northern Mexican towns. Officials from the Mexican government looked around for new ways to employ the excess labor their economy could otherwise not absorb. They found what they wanted in Asia in the concept of global production sharing. According to this concept, labor-intensive products manufactured in high wage, developed countries could be more efficiently assembled in low wage, developing countries, thereby providing jobs and foreign exchange for the developing economies.

In 1965, the Mexican government implemented the Programa de Industrialización Fronteriza (Border Industrialization Program or BIP), which mainly promoted the establishment of maquiladoras in the region. This program provided for duty-free importation of machinery and component parts for assembly (inputs) as long as the final product was re-exported. It also allowed for up to 100% foreign ownership of the manufacturing operation at a time when Mexico's rules for foreign investment stipulated that foreigners must hold a minority position in any project. Finally, maquiladoras were not liable for any Mexican income tax since they typically did not generate sales in Mexico. Given this last factor, along with the market-oriented trade and investment provisions under the maquiladora program and Mexico's accessible labor, the country surfaced as a very attractive export platform for multinational firms, especially U.S. corporations. This program was facilitated by favorable U.S. tax treatment where only the value added in Mexico was taxed, which was mainly the cost of labor.

As the Mexican economy slowed and began to experience structural problems in the late 1970s, and then again in the early 1980s, peso devaluations became commonplace. The cost of Mexican labor thus fell dramatically in comparison with other export platform countries, especially Asia.[6] During the 1980s, the maquiladora industry grew rapidly and became the main source of new jobs in Mexico and one of the leading generators of foreign exchange. Non–U.S. firms, mostly Asian, were also attracted to the maquiladora program by the lower wages and the possibility of gaining access to the North American market. By manufacturing and assembling in Mexico, foreign firms could obtain duty-free entry of their exports into the U.S. market, as long as a certain minimum percentage of the total value of the product was added in Mexico.

During the 1980s and early 1990s, the state of Baja California, on the far western part of the border, became a major center for the production of television sets by Japanese firms. The prospect of a North American Free Trade Agreement (NAFTA) stimulated additional Asian investment in this state and elsewhere along the border. During the same period, dynamic maquiladora investment turned the state of Chihuahua into a stronghold for major U.S. automakers. As Mexico added more free-trade agreements with Latin American countries and, more recently, with the European Union, the incentives for multinational firms to invest in the country—low wages and taxes and an absence of independent labor unions—were greater than ever. Consequently, by 2000, approximately 1.3 million workers were employed in the maquiladora industry, of whom 82.7%, (about 1.02 million workers) were living in the border states. The assembly-manufacturing sector had become one of the main drivers, if not the main driver, of the Mexican border economy.

The growth of the maquiladora industry often resulted in the loss of U.S. jobs in basic manufacturing, although maquiladora production simultaneously created jobs for U.S. industries that produce the inputs imported by maquiladoras. Communities along the U.S.–Mexican border have regarded the expansion of the maquiladora sector as a source of jobs, incomes, and tax revenue. They argue that as Mexican border communities attract assembly-manufacturing firms and jobs, and as incomes on the Mexican side expand, those firms and their employees frequently buy goods and services on the U.S. side. Maquiladoras often establish warehouse, transportation, communication, and office facilities on the U.S. side. Also, some managers and technical staff of the maquiladoras reside in U.S. border communities with their families. In recent years, manufacturing facilities that feed components to the plants on the Mexican side have been set up in the United States.[7] NAFTA has begun to change some of these relationships. Under the agreement, U.S. retail firms are better able to expand into Mexico, which, eventually, should reduce some of the cross-border retail trade referred to above. In addition, the specific legal framework behind the maquiladora program is essentially phased out by NAFTA. However, the maquiladora plants as an industrial base will remain, albeit under new regulations and procedures.[8]

While providing for dramatic steps toward increased free trade and substantially opening Mexico to foreign investment, NAFTA did not provide for cross-border labor flows. There have been pressures recently to include labor mobility in the NAFTA region. According to a press release from the office of the President of Mexico, at the first meeting of Vincente Fox and George W. Bush in February 2001, this subject was given special attention and a working group was established to engage in "formal high-level negotiations aimed at achieving short- and long-term agreements that will allow us to constructively address migration and labor issues between our two countries."

The above discussion underlines the great degree of economic interdependence that exists among the U.S. and Mexican border communities. This is especially true of the maquiladora sector. As will be discussed later, the rapid growth of employment in the maquiladora sector has had a very favorable impact on retail sales in U.S. border communities. Maquiladora wages create purchasing power that is used, at least in part, to make purchases in the United States. The vitality of the maquiladora sector is also dependent on the dynamics of the U.S. economy. While the U.S. economy boomed in the 1990s, demand for products produced by maquiladoras also boomed. This demand, combined with the 1994 peso devaluation, created a powerful combination of forces driving the growth of the sector. Maquiladoras rapidly increased in number and size. In 1994, there were approximately 2,085 maquiladoras operating in Mexico. By 2000, this number had mushroomed to 3,590. In addition, many existing maquiladoras expanded operations. This growth did not immediately convert into increased retail sales across the border. In fact, because the devaluation meant that peso salaries lost purchasing power in terms of dollars, retail sales actually fell in U.S. border towns. As the Mexican economy recovered, U.S. retail sales also rebounded. In 2001, as the U.S. economy began to slow, the demand for maquiladora products declined and this was reflected in significant cutbacks in employment at some maquiladoras. Thus, the interdependence of the economies of the border communities is very apparent. It is not likely that employment in the maquiladora sector will fully recover until the U.S. economy returns to full vitality.

In summary, the concepts of complementarity and interdependence provide the basis for understanding the economic and demographic expansion that the border region has experienced, especially in the last four decades. While cross-border trade and commerce—stimulated by high Mexican tariffs—were the main drivers of these characteristics until the mid-1980s, cross-border assembly and manufacturing activities have become dominant in the last 15 years due to lower wages and the advantages associated with the maquiladora program and NAFTA. NAFTA provisions provide for the phase-out of all tariff as well as most nontariff barriers to exports, imports, and local border transactions, while barriers to foreign investment will also be reduced dramatically. As prices and availability of consumer goods on both sides of the border tend to converge, the level of local border transactions can be expected to diminish in relative terms while assembly and manufacturing activities and the degree of cross-border integration in those sectors is likely to increase.

U.S. Border Communities Profiles

Each community in the U.S.–Mexican border region is unique in terms of its population size, economic structure, and its relationship with the community on the other side of the border. There is, however, one factor that each of these communities share. Their economic and environmental situations are linked with those of their neighbors, and therefore, decision-making processes must take these transborder spillover effects into account for development of sound public policy. Table 1 provides data on 2000 population and 1999 personal incomes for seven U.S. metropolitan statistical areas (MSAs) located along the border region and are compared with the four U.S. border states and the United States as a whole.

Table 1. U.S. Border Region: Population and Personal Income

	Population	Personal Income 1999	
Area	2000	Per Capita	Percent of National Average
San Diego, CA	2,813,833	29,489	103.3
Yuma, AZ	160,026	18,452	64.6
Las Cruces, NM	174,682	17,003	59.6
El Paso, TX	679,522	17,216	60.3
Laredo, TX	193,117	14,112	49.4
McAllen, TX	569,463	13,339	46.7
Brownsville, TX	335,227	14,280	50.0
Non–MSA Border	1,370,627		
Border Total	6,296,497		
California	33,871,648	29,856	104.6
Arizona	5,130,632	25,173	88.2
New Mexico	1,819,046	21,836	76.5
Texas	20,851,820	26,834	94.0
United States	281,421,906	28,546	100.0

Sources: U.S. Census Bureau, Census (2000); U.S. Department of Commerce, Bureau of Economic Analysis (n.d.).

California Border Communities

California has the largest population of any state in the United States. The total population of California was 33.87 million in 2000 and the population of its two border counties, San Diego and Imperial, represented about 8.7% of the total state population, with approximately 2.8 and 0.14 million inhabitants, respectively.

From an economic perspective, California's two border counties are quite different from one another. San Diego's economy is much larger and more diverse than any other U.S. border community, with a highly educated labor force, modern high-tech industries, and the highest per capita personal income of any border county—$29,489 in 1999. Traditionally, San Diego's economy has been heavily dependent on military expenditures, with its large marine and navy bases as well as a strong aerospace industry. However, since the end of the Cold War, San Diego's economy has become more diversified, specializing in the biotechnology and pharmaceutical industries, telecommunications, computer and electronic manufacturing, medical services, software and computer services, and visitor services such as hotels, restaurants, and entertainment and amusement industries.

Imperial County has historically specialized in agribusiness, but in recent years the economy has become more diversified. The construction of two new large federal prisons in the county and the increase in NAFTA–related commercial traffic have been significant economic developments. Nevertheless, Imperial County is a much more typical border community in terms of per capita personal income and unemployment rates. In 1998, Imperial County had an unemployment rate of 26.3% and a per capita income of $17,353.

Despite their border location, the impact of Mexico on these communities, especially in San Diego, is miniscule in comparison with the impact of the Los Angeles basin and the rest of California. For example, in 1990, Mexico accounted only for 6.2% of San Diego's total international and domestic exports to other regions of the United States (Rey et al. 1998).

Arizona Border Communities

Relative to its neighbor, California, Arizona is a small state. However, Arizona is experiencing rapid demographic growth. In 2000, its population reached 5.13 million, an increase of 40% relative to 1990. About 35% of Arizona's residents are concentrated in the cities of Phoenix and Tucson. Tucson is closest to the border, but at a distance of approximately 60 miles it cannot be considered a typical border community.

Much of the rest of the state is rural and sparsely populated. The rural economy is dominated by agriculture, while Phoenix and Tucson have become centers of high tech economic activity. Arizona's main economic sectors include services, trade, and manufacturing. Mining and agriculture are also important, although they tend to be more capital intensive than labor intensive. The service sector is the single largest employer statewide. Arizona's per capita personal income was estimated to be $25,173 in 1999. Yuma County, a border county, had a per capita personal income of $18,452 in the same year.

The city of Yuma, the population center of Yuma County, is the largest Arizona city within 20 miles of the border with Mexico. In 2000, the county had a population of 160,026, of which 77,515 resided in the city. Tourism is a major contributor to the Yuma regional economy (22–25% of total output). Spending by winter visitors from the northern United States and from Canada accounts for most of this tourism revenue. The municipality of San Luis Río Colorado, Sonora, which borders Yuma County, also benefits from this influx. From October to March, the population of Yuma County swells to about 215,000 with winter visitors, contributing to the vitality of the entire retail sector and bolstering sales tax revenues significantly. Agriculture and government services represent the other two main drivers of the Yuma economy. High tech, irrigated agriculture generates $700 to $800 million in gross revenues annually, the largest share (35–40%) of the output of the county. The Marine Corps Air Station and Yuma Proving Grounds represent the chief sources of revenue in the government sector, which produces another 18–20% of regional output. The seasonal fluctuations of jobs in the two key sectors of tourism and agriculture result in serious seasonal unemployment for Yuma County, which often reaches 30%.

In 2000, with approximately 21,000 residents, the city of Nogales was a relatively small Arizona border community in comparison with other U.S.–Mexican border cities. In 2000, Nogales accounted for 54.4% of the total population of Santa Cruz County, one of the smallest counties in Arizona. Yet, Nogales is the largest of Arizona's six ports-of-entry into Mexico, accounting for more than 60% of commercial and pedestrian traffic moving across the Arizona–Sonora border. Because of close economic and cultural ties between Nogales, Arizona, and Nogales, Sonora, they are often referred to as Ambos Nogales.

Nogales is the principal port-of-entry for fresh produce from Mexico and it handles more than 60% of all winter vegetables and fruits shipped from Mexico to U.S. and Canadian markets. More than $5 billion worth of vegetables and fruits cross the border into the United States each year at Nogales, Arizona. The city's retail sector is heavily dependent on cross-border shopping by residents from the adjacent twin city of Nogales, Sonora. An expanding maquiladora sector south of the border has spurred a wide variety of new jobs in manufacturing and services.

A large part of the Nogales, Arizona, labor force is employed in trade (40% of total employment) and government (23%). Services provide jobs for another 15% of workers, while manufacturing employs 9% of the labor force. The seasonal character of the fresh produce industry is largely responsible for high unemployment rates, reaching over 20% in the county and over 25% in the city.

Nogale's is favorably positioned where U.S. Interstate 19 meets Mexican Federal Highway 15. The railroad crossing, one of the oldest along the U.S.–Mexican border, connects the Union Pacific with the Mexican Ferrocarril del Pacífico (Pacific Railroad). Currently, it is utilized for shipment of auto parts to the Ford Company in Hermosillo, Sonora, and assembled cars back to the United States.

New Mexico Border Communities

Demographically, New Mexico is a very small state with a population in 2000 of only 1.82 million. It is also the poorest of the four border states with a per capita personal income of $21,836 in 1999, 76.5% of the national average.

Since New Mexico has only three small ports of entry with no significant urbanized area on the border and a relatively low volume of trade with Mexico, it was not included in the survey.[9] However, there are some developments along the New Mexico–Mexico border that provide the infrastructure for future population growth and trade. A relatively new port of entry, Santa Teresa–San Jerónimo, has been opened just to the west of El Paso, Texas. The port now has cattle pens and commercial and noncommercial inspection facilities. A paved highway recently connected the port with the southern part of Ciudad Juárez and there is now a four-lane highway that links Santa Teresa with the U.S. interstate highway system. Since the Santa Teresa–San Jerónimo crossing avoids the densely populated and congested urban areas of Ciudad Juárez and El Paso, it is likely that commercial truck crossings will increase dramatically at this New Mexico port.

Texas Border Communities

Texas is, geographically, the largest state in the United States and shares the longest border with Mexico. Sixteen of the 25 U.S. border counties are located in Texas. An important consideration regarding NAFTA is that a very large proportion—approximately 80%—of all land trade between the United States and Mexico passes through Texas counties, with approximately 38% coming through the city of Laredo alone.

Of the total population of Texas in 2000 (20.85 million), approximately 9.5% lived in the 16 counties immediately adjacent to the U.S.–Mexican border. Many differences exist between the border counties and interior counties of Texas. One of the most significant is a lower high school graduation rate in border counties. Given this, it is not surprising that per capita personal income at the border is lower than in the rest of the state. In 1999, the state's per capita personal income was $26,834, while El Paso had a per capita personal income of $17,216; Laredo, $14,112; McAllen, $13,339; and Brownsville, $14,280.

The largest metropolitan statistical area (MSA) in the Texas border region is El Paso. El Paso County, located in the western part of the state, had 679,522 inhabitants in 2000. Among the various segments of the El Paso services sectors that are expanding, several directly reflect the emerging commercial and industrial linkages to Ciudad Juárez and other regions of Mexico. For example, international air traffic through El Paso continues to expand, as do northbound bridge crossings. Much of the latter is a function of increased maquiladora investment throughout the state of Chihuahua.

Laredo County, which is located toward the middle of the Texas border area, had a 2000 population of 193,117, and nearby Eagle Pass is one of the smallest cities with a population of 22,413. The two MSAs located in the Rio Grande Valley in the eastern part of the state are Brownsville–Harlingen–San Benito and McAllen–Edinburg–Mission with populations of approximately 335,227 and 569,463, respectively.

Over the last decade, population growth in the Texas border region has been very high, outpacing the state's average by nearly two to one. Between 1990 and 1999, the population growth of these communities averaged about 32%, compared to 18% for the state of Texas as a whole. The expansion in U.S.–Mexican trade, cross-border commerce, and investment during the 1990s have been the driving forces behind the explosive growth taking place in the Texas border region. The economies of Texas border communities, large and small, are rooted in trade and service activities with Mexico. Cross-border wholesale/retail, services, and transshipment services (warehousing and transportation) represent a larger share of Laredo's, Brownsville's, and Eagle Pass's economic activity relative to the more diversified economies of El Paso and McAllen. Nevertheless, the welfare of all Texas border communities is more directly determined by the ups and downs of the Mexican economy than by the performance of their own state or national economies.

Mexican Border Communities Profiles

Table 2 provides 2000 population and maquiladora information for major border cities and border states.

Baja California Border Communities

Baja California has the largest border population of all the northern border states and has grown more rapidly than any other Mexican border state in recent years. In 2000, the population of the state's three border municipalities accounted for 82.5% of its entire population. From 1995 to 2000, the state's population increased by approximately 18%, from 2,112,140 to 2,487,367 inhabitants. However, the rate of growth has decreased from 8% annually during the 1960s to 5% in the 1990s.

Almost half (48.7%) of the state's population lives in Tijuana, which in 2000 had a population of 1,210,820. While unemployment in the area is estimated to be quite low—1.1% in 2000—many Tijuana residents cross the international border to find more remunerative jobs. Some residents are U.S. citizens or permanent U.S. residents who live in Tijuana because of lower housing costs. A December 1995 commuter survey indicated a daily crossing of 18,980 workers at the San Ysidro port of entry,[10] of whom 17,535 were U.S. residents. The most recent figures for Tijuana showed that approximately 7% of the jobs held by Tijuana's economically active residents are located in the United States.

Tijuana income levels are significantly above the state and national averages for family, per capita, and household income in 1995.[11] Per

Table 2: Mexican Border Region Population and Maquiladora Employment, 2000

	Population		Maquiladoras		Employment in Maquiladoras	
Cities	Total 2000 Population	Percent of State	Total Number of Plants	Mexico Total Percent	Total Number of Workers	Percent of Local Economically Active Population
Tijuana	1,210,820	48.7	788	21.9	187,339	36
Mexicali	764,602	30.7	194	5.4	60,063	19
Ciudad Juárez	1,218,817	39.9	308	8.6	249,509	48
Nuevo Laredo	310,915	11.3	54	1.5	22,603	18
Matamoros	418,141	15.2	119	3.3	66,023	35
States		Percent of State's Population Living in Border Cities				Percent of Maquiladora Workers
Baja California	2,487,367	82.5	1,218	33.9	274,581	21.4
Sonora	2,216,969	23.3	284	7.9	105,391	8.2
Chihuahua	3,052,907	42.5	446	12.4	318,957	24.8
Coahuila	2,298,070	12.5	280	7.8	114,032	8.9
Nuevo León	3,834,141	0.5	156	4.3	68,261	5.3
Tamaulipas	2,753,222	50.2	375	10.4	181,150	14.1
Total Border States	16,642,676	33.0	2,759	76.9	1,062,372	82.7
Other States	80,840,736		831	23.1	222,635	17.3
Mexico	97,483,412	5.7	3,590	100.0	1,285,007	100.0

Source: INEGI (2001); Características de la Industria Maquiladora de Exportación (2000).

capita income, for example, was 32% higher than the statewide average and 1.2% higher than the national average in that year.

Because of its proximity to the international border, Tijuana's economy is quite integrated into the California and U.S. economy. Maquiladoras, wholesale trade, retail trade, transportation, and tourism provide most of the city's jobs. In 2000, Tijuana's 788 maquiladoras employed nearly 187,400 workers, mainly in the electric appliances, electronic components, apparel, textiles, and metal mechanics sectors. Maquiladora employment in Tijuana increased steadily at an average rate of 14.1% per year during the 1995–2000 period. In 2001, as the recession in the United States deepened, maquiladora employment in Tijuana showed some downturn.

Tecate and Mexicali are the other main border municipalities in Baja California, with populations in 2000 of 77,795 and 764,602, respectively. The municipality of Mexicali is a major producer of agricultural and horticultural products and the output of these products is increasing. Most of the manufacturing activity in Tecate and Mexicali is related to the maquiladora industry. In 2000, Tecate had 138 maquiladora plants that employed over 12,100 workers. Mexicali has a large maquiladora sector with 194 plants and over 60,000 workers in 2000. Other major employment sectors include services, construction, transportation, and public utilities.

Sonora Border Communities

In 2000, the state of Sonora had a total population of 2,216,969 with more than one quarter (27.5%) living in the city of Hermosillo, 180 miles south of the international border. Sonora's border population, which in 2000 accounted for 23.3% of the state's population, is mainly concentrated in Agua Prieta, Nogales, and San Luis Río Colorado, with populations in 2000 of 61,944, 159,787, and 145,006, respectively. Unemployment rates in the three cities appear to have remained at the 3–4% level during the past few years. Nogales has the lowest unemployment rate, and provides more than one-third of the state's jobs and most of the recent employment growth. Employment growth in Nogales during 1994–2000 in just the maquiladora sector was more than 98%, increasing from a monthly average of 19,503 workers in 1994 to a monthly average of 38,633 in 2000.

Sonora is a rich agricultural state. Irrigated croplands provide field crops and ranching provides livestock products, including some dairy products. About one-third of the irrigated cropland is adjacent to the Colorado River in San Luis Río Colorado, which itself accounts for about 95% of the total value of products sold by the three border cities. It was also the only border city to show significant growth in agricultural output between 1990 and 1995.

Manufacturing is not well developed in Sonora's border except for the maquiladora industry, which generates an important number of jobs in Agua Prieta, Nogales, and San Luis Río Colorado. In 2000, maquiladora annual average employment in Agua Prieta was nearly 7,600 in 34 plants, Nogales had nearly 38,700 workers in 90 plants, and San Luis Río Colorado had nearly 11,500 workers in 39 plants. Other major employment sectors include services, construction, transportation, communications, public utilities, and wholesale trade. With the exception of services, most of these sectors recorded very little employment growth during the 1990–1995 period.

Chihuahua Border Communities

Chihuahua, with a population of 3,052,907 in 2000, has the second largest population of the Mexican border states. People living along the border accounted for 42.5% of Chihuahua's population. Most of the population of Chihuahua lives in the border city of Ciudad Juárez (40%), which alone has four border crossings. Other Chihuahua border crossings into the United States are located in Ojinaga, San Jerónimo, and Palomas, yet they are quite small and relatively insignificant in terms of cross-border traffic. The city of Chihuahua, in the southern part of the state, is the only other large urban area with a population of 671,790.

Ciudad Juárez, with population of 1,218,817 in 2000, serves as an important retail, commercial, and tourist center for U.S. citizens, and is an important port of entry for U.S. tourists and U.S. goods entering Mexico. The city is also the focal point for maquiladora operations and is an important distribution center for the state of Chihuahua and the interior of Mexico.

Maquiladora employment in Ciudad Juárez totaled more than 249,500 in 2000, providing some 50% of all jobs in the city's formal sector. Maquiladora employment in Ciudad Juárez grew at an average annual rate of 10.1% during the 1995–2000 period. Of the 308 maquiladora plants registered in 2000, many were quite large, with more than 500 employees, and were owned by Fortune 500 firms in the United States. Automotive and electronics are the industry's dominant sectors in Ciudad Juárez. For example, Delphi Automotive—a company that until 1999 was part of General Motors and is Mexico's largest private-sector employer—has a considerable presence in Ciudad Juárez. It has 15 manufacturing facilities in the city and, in 1995, set up a technical center dedicated to the research and design of auto parts used by the world's top automakers. The technical center employs some 2,000 workers, most of them engineers. Thomson Consumer Electronics and Valeo (formerly ITT) have also opened technical centers in Ciudad Juárez, indicating that this city has positioned itself as a leader at the highest end of maquiladora investment that includes research and development.

Ojinaga, with a population of 24,307 in 2000, has an economy similar to that of Presidio, Texas, being predominantly a farm and ranch supply/distribution center. Ojinaga, however, does have a small maquiladora industry presence. In 2000, the city had eight plants employing 967 workers.

Coahuila Border Communities

In 2000, Coahuila's population was 2,298,070. The state's population increased 16.5% from 1990 to 2000, compared to a 26.6% increase from 1980 to 1990. Despite these increases, out-migration from the state has been continuous in recent years. The net loss from 1980 to 1990 was 68,785 and from 1990 to 1995 it was estimated at 102,000. Most of the population is concentrated in a number of cities in the southern part of the state, of which Saltillo, with a population of 578,046 in 2000, is the largest. Torreón with a population of 529,512 and Monclova with 193,744 are the next largest communities. Along the border, Piedras Negras with a population of 128,130 and Ciudad Acuña with 110,487 in 2000 are the largest communities. Only 12.5% of the state's population lives directly on the U.S.–Mexican border.

From 1985 to 1995, employment in Coahuila fell by more than 20%, due almost entirely to the reduced demand for steel.[12] This industry has been seriously affected since the beginning of trade liberalization in 1986.

The border municipalities of Piedras Negras and Ciudad Acuña are the only urban areas in the state to experience population increases, due perhaps to the rising employment in the retail trade sector—the largest single employment sector in the two cities. Per capita retail sales there were much higher than in other border cities, indicative of cross-border spending by Americans.

In 2000, Piedras Negras had 38 maquiladora plants that employed over 14,500 workers, while Ciudad Acuña had 56 plants with more than 32,100 workers. Most of the maquiladora plants are involved in the assembly of electrical and electronic items.

Nuevo León Border Communities

Nuevo León, the most industrialized of the five border states, has no significant port of entry to the United States and there are no large towns on the U.S. side of the border. In 2000, only 0.5% of the state's population lived in Anáhuac, the only municipality in the state of Nuevo León adjacent to the border. Two-thirds of the population live in six municipalities located in the central-southern section of the state, of which Monterrey, with a 2000 population of 1,110,997, is the largest.

Concerned about the lack of a port of entry in the state, Nuevo León's government and the private sector have pushed for a border crossing for many years. Eventually, the Solidarity Bridge was opened across the Rio Grande near Columbia, Nuevo León. The government of Nuevo León constructed a modern highway connecting this port of entry with Monterrey and other industrial centers in the state. A private toll road, Camino Columbia, built west of Laredo, Texas, in 2000 connects the Columbia-Solidarity Bridge to I-35 21 miles north of Laredo.

Tamaulipas Border Communities

In 2000, the state of Tamaulipas had a population of 2,753,222, of which 50.2% lived in border municipalities. Three metropolitan areas accounted for 83% of the state's border population (1,382,212) in 2000. Reynosa is the largest municipality with a population of 420,463 in 2000. Matamoros, located on the Gulf of Mexico, is the second largest with a population of 418,141, and Nuevo Laredo is the third largest with a population of 310,915. The economies of Nuevo

Laredo, Matamoros, and Reynosa depend heavily on their proximity to the border with the United States. Wholesale trade, retail trade, transportation, and tourism provide most of these cities' jobs.

Nuevo Laredo is a major gateway for international trade and tourism with the United States. It is the largest inland port in the nation and its retail merchants enjoy one of the highest per capita retail sales rates in Mexico. In 2000, 8.3 million vehicles and 11.4 million pedestrians crossed into Mexico from the United States through Laredo. Reynosa is a principal farm product supply distribution center. Reynosa's largest single employer is a large petrochemical complex operated by the Mexican national petroleum company PEMEX.

Matamoros serves as an important retail, commercial, and tourism center for U.S. citizens. Almost 10 million persons annually enter Mexico through Brownsville, and a thriving retail/tourist trade augments the city's diverse economy. The city has a large maquiladora sector and is an important distribution center for the state and the interior of Mexico. The other border municipalities of Tamaulipas have large maquiladora sectors. In 2000, Matamoros had 119 plants employing 66,023 workers. Reynosa, however, has been growing at a faster rate than Matamoros in recent years. During the 1995–2000 period, Reynosa's maquiladora employment grew at an average annual rate of 10.3%; the corresponding figure for Matamoros was 8.2%. In 2000, Reynosa had 117 plants (two less than in Matamoros) with a workforce of 66,091, slightly higher than the Matamoros total. However, compared to Matamoros and Reynosa, Nuevo Laredo does not have a large maquiladora sector. In 2000, it had only 54 plants employing slightly more than 22,600 workers—just 2% of the industry's national total.

III

Changing Demographic and Economic Patterns in the U.S.–Mexican Border Region during the NAFTA Era

As noted in the introduction to this study, given the many factors influencing the region's evolution during the last decade, NOBE/REF researchers decided that it would be extremely difficult to isolate the effects of NAFTA itself. Such an endeavor would not only require considerable resources, but would suffer from a lack of consistent data for the two countries at the municipal level. As an alternative, it was decided to analyze published data and existing studies to identify the main demographic and economic changes in the border region in the context of the changes occurring at the national level in the two countries.[13]

What follows is a summary of existing data on the changing economic and demographic situation in the U.S.–Mexican border region during the NAFTA era. This time period is loosely defined and depends mainly on data availability. However, it roughly coincides with the decade of the 1990s. In order to put the data on the border region in context, comparisons with other time periods and with the situation in border states and/or the two nations as a whole are made where relevant.

EXPANSION OF ECONOMIC ACTIVITY IN THE 1990S

Since it is difficult to precisely summarize the dramatic increase in economic activity in the U.S.–Mexican border region during the NAFTA era, some illustrative data provide examples of trends. Indicators regarding bilateral trade, investment flows, maquiladora employment, and cross-border transportation provide good examples of economic activity during the NAFTA era.

Stimulated by dramatically lower tariff rates in Mexico beginning in the late 1980s and by NAFTA tariff reductions beginning in 1994, total U.S.–Mexican trade increased by 141% between 1993 and 1999 (Vargas 2000a). Since most of the U.S.–Mexican trade moves across the land border, it is not surprising that between 1990 and 1999 southbound truck crossings from Texas into Mexico (where a large proportion of U.S.–Mexican trade crosses the international boundary) increased by 278%, while rail car crossings increased by 179% (Texas Center for Border Economic and Enterprise Development 2001)

Reforms in the Mexican economy and the new NAFTA rules accounted for increasing foreign investment, particularly after the implementation of the trade agreement. Before the implementation of NAFTA (1988–1993), annual flows to Mexico of total foreign direct investment (FDI) averaged $3.7 billion; however, after NAFTA's implementation, during the 1994–1998 period they averaged $11.4 billion, an increase of over 300% (Vargas 2000a).

Border manufacturing also experienced growth in the NAFTA era. Stimulated by falling wage rates associated with the peso devaluation in December 1994 and new NAFTA investment rules, the number of workers in border maquiladoras increased by 88.4% between 1994 and 2000, compared to only 14.5% in the 1989–1993 period. However, this growth was exceeded by maquiladora expansion in the interior of Mexico. Maquiladora employment in the interior grew 205% during 1994–2000 compared to growth of 70.1% during 1989–1993. The growth of this sector in the interior was stimulated by factors such as better labor availability, lower labor costs, improving transportation infrastructure, and investment incentives offered by state and local governments.

THE CHANGING U.S. BORDER REGION IN THE 1990S

Tables 3 and 4, compiled by James Peach (Peach and Adkisson 2000), provide a succinct overview of the eight metropolitan statistical areas (MSAs) located in the U.S. border region and are compared with the four U.S. border states and the United States as a whole.[14] These eight MSAs comprise more than 90% of the border region's population. The data in these two tables illustrate a number of important characteristics of the U.S. border region.

Table 3. U.S. Border Region: Selected Characteristics

	Population		Income 1997		Labor Force		
Area	1998 (1,000s)	Percent Change (1990–98)	Per Capita	Percent of Nation	Participation Rate 1990	Unemployment Rate 1998	High School Percent*
San Diego, CA	2,780.6	10.6	24,965	98.7	68.4	3.5	81.9
Yuma, AZ	132.3	22.8	15,629	61.8	59.0	27.9	64.9
Tucson, AZ	790.8	18.3	21,068	83.3	61.8	2.7	80.5
Las Cruces, NM	169.2	23.9	14,923	59.0	60.5	8.5	70.4
El Paso, TX	703.1	18.0	15,216	60.2	61.3	10.2	63.7
Laredo, TX	188.2	39.9	12,999	51.4	57.7	9.2	47.8
McAllen, TX	522.2	35.0	12,005	47.5	55.0	17.7	46.6
Brownsville, TX	326.4	24.7	12,857	50.8	53.0	9.2	50.0
Non–MSA Border	525.6	23.2	15,123	59.8	56.1	18.6	57.5
Border Total	6,138.3	17.3	20,376	78.2	63.5	7.6	74.1
California	32,666.5	9.2	26,218	103.7	67.0	3.5	76.2
Arizona	4,668.6	26.9	21,996	87.0	62.9	4.1	78.7
New Mexico	1,736.9	14.3	19,249	76.1	62.8	6.2	75.1
Texas	19,759.6	15.9	23,647	93.5	66.0	4.8	72.1
United States	270,438.7	8.4	25,288	100.0	65.3	4.5	75.2

*Percent of population 25 years old or older with a high school diploma.

Sources: (1) Population estimates are from U.S. Bureau of the Census, November, 1999. (2) Per Capita Income estimates from U.S. Department of Commerce, Bureau of Economic Analysis, 1999. (3) Labor Force Participation Rates calculated from U.S. Bureau of the Census, 1993. (4) Unemployment rates from U.S. Bureau of Labor Statistics, 1999. (5) Percent High School graduates calculated from U.S. Bureau of the Census, 1993.

Table 4. U.S. Border Region: Selected Growth Indicators

	Average Annual Percent Change in Population		Average Annual Percent Change in Per Capita Income		Percent Change in Employment		Unemployment Rate	
Area	1990–93	1994–98	1990–93	1994–97	1990–93	1994–98	1993	1998
San Diego, CA	1.28	1.46	1.57	3.35	-0.40	2.60	7.7	3.5
Yuma, AZ	3.50	2.53	3.83	2.26	1.40	1.96	27.8	27.9
Tucson, AZ	2.16	1.92	3.30	3.19	1.54	1.32	4.0	2.7
Las Cruces, NM	3.77	2.10	2.34	2.38	0.88	2.18	8.6	8.5
El Paso, TX	2.63	1.59	2.84	3.02	2.72	0.48	10.8	10.2
Laredo, TX	5.36	3.81	5.46	2.53	5.78	1.84	10.5	9.2
McAllen, TX	4.69	3.35	3.07	3.01	2.86	2.23	20.6	17.7
Brownsville, TX	3.36	2.47	4.01	2.35	3.86	1.12	13.5	9.2
Non–MSA Border	3.96	1.74	2.03	1.94	2.61	0.16	20.4	18.6
Border Counties	2.33	1.87	2.99	2.74	0.99	1.86	10.2	7.6
California	1.34	1.10	1.25	3.66	-0.94	2.13	7.7	3.5
Arizona	2.85	3.14	2.50	3.75	0.29	3.76	6.3	4.1
New Mexico	2.09	1.26	3.59	3.13	1.80	1.70	7.7	6.2
Texas	1.89	1.92	3.35	4.18	1.76	2.28	7.2	4.8
United States	1.11	0.96	2.69	3.66	0.41	1.67	6.9	4.5

Sources: See Table 3.

The demographic dynamism of the border region is remarkable. The total population of U.S. border counties increased by 17.3% during the 1990–1998 period. This was almost double the 8.4% increase for the United States as a whole (Peach and Adkisson 2000).[15] While population growth for this period is well above the national average, the same is not true for other characteristics. Labor force participation rates and high school graduation rates in the border region are generally lower than in the United States as a whole, while unemployment is higher. San Diego, however, is the exception to these trends.

Before the implementation of NAFTA, during the 1990–1993 period, annual employment growth along the border was more than twice the national average at 1% for the border and 0.4% for the nation. During the 1994–1998 period, employment growth in the border region was 1.9%, which was only slightly higher than the nation at 1.7%. However, since total population growth in the border was double the national average for the entire period (1990–1998), the border was still able to roughly maintain its position with respect to the nation in the pre–NAFTA era, but fell farther behind in the NAFTA era. Unemployment figures for the period between 1994 and 1998 are consistent with the employment data. In this period, unemployment in U.S. border counties fell by 25%, significantly less than the nation as a whole, which declined by 35%.

While per capita incomes vary considerably within the border region (for example, in 1999, San Diego had a per capita personal income of $29,489, while McAllen only had $13,339), with the exception of San Diego, they are all lower than the U.S. average of $28,546 (see Table 1). This situation was not improved by NAFTA. Prior to NAFTA (1990–1993), per capita income growth in the U.S. border region (2.9%) was slightly higher than the national figure (2.7%). However, during the 1994–1997 period, income growth in the border region (2.7%) was significantly lower than the annual national average growth of 3.6% during the same period (see Table 4).

The Changing Mexican Border Region in the 1990s

While the U.S. border region lagged behind U.S. averages in indicators other than population, the situation in the Mexican border area was quite different. Like the northern side of the boundary, the Mexican border area showed significant demographic dynamism. Over the entire 1990–2000 period, Mexico's national population increased by 23.7%, while growth in the border municipalities was almost twice as high at 40.7%. From 1990 to 1995, the annual population growth rate of the Mexican border region was approximately 1.5 percentage points higher than for the nation as a whole (3.5% versus 2.3%). During the period from 1995 to 2000, the annual rate was almost two percentage points higher than the nation as a whole, at 3.6% versus 1.8%.

People in the Mexican border region, in contrast to the situation north of the boundary, are somewhat better educated than the nation as a whole. In 1995, 6.6% of the border region population had a university education, compared to 5.4% for Mexico as a whole.

With the rapid population growth in Mexico's border region, there was also significant expansion of employment. Between 1990 and 1994, employment grew annually by 4.5% at the national level in

Table 5. Mexico and its Border States: Selected Characteristics

	Mexico	Border Region
Population Growth (annual rate)		
1990–1995	2.3	3.5
1995–2000	1.8	3.6
Employment Growth (annual rate)		
1990–1994	4.5	5.9
1994–1997	4.7	6.8
Percentage of Work Force Earning < Minimum Wage		
1990–1994	8.5	6.0
1994–1998	11.2	4.4
Percentage of Population with University Education		
1990	5.1	6.2
1995	5.4	6.6
Unemployment Rate (urban areas)		
1990	2.7	2.1
1995	6.3	3.5
2000	2.3	1.2
Real GDP Growth Rate		
1993–1995	-0.8	0.8
1996–1998	7.4	5.9
Employment Percentage in Manufacturing		
1992	22.0	21.2
1998	22.2	32.6
Per Capita GDP (1,000s of 1993 Pesos)		
1990	13.8	15.3
1995	12.4	16.0
2000	14.2	19.6

Source: INEGI data for several years compiled by El Colegio de la Frontera Norte (COLEF).

Mexico, compared to 5.9% in the border region, a difference of 1.4 percentage points. During the 1994–1997 period, the difference in annual growth rates rose by more than two percentage points (4.7% versus 6.8%). Despite the rapid expansion of the border population, unemployment rates throughout the 1990s were significantly lower in the border region compared to the nation as a whole. The disparity between the border region and the nation was not as marked as it was during Mexico's severe recession in 1995. Clearly, Mexico's border benefited from the strong U.S. economy during the 1995 downturn. Within the Mexican border region, the lowest unemployment rates are usually found in Tijuana, Ciudad Juárez, and Nuevo Laredo, while Matamoros usually has the highest rates.

In terms of wages, the Mexican border region was also relatively better off than the nation as a whole. For example, from 1990 to 1994, the proportion of workers earning less than the minimum wage in the border municipalities was less than 6%, compared to 8.5% for Mexico as a whole. During the 1994–1998 period, the situation in the border region improved somewhat as the proportion of the workers earning less than the minimum wage dropped to less than 4.4%. However, at the national level, the situation got worse, increasing from 8.5% to approximately 11.2%.

At the macro level, gross regional product (GRP) in the Mexican border region grew only slightly faster than gross domestic product (GDP), despite significantly higher employment growth. In 1993–1995 and 1996–1998, GRP growth in the border region was almost two percentage points higher than in the nation as a whole (0.8% versus -0.8% and 7.4% versus 5.9%, respectively). Additionally, per capita GRP in the border region grew faster than per capita GDP in the country as a whole. Consequently, the per capita GDP gap between the border region and the country as a whole is widening. In 2000, the GDP per capita in Mexico as a whole was $14,200 pesos versus GRP per capita of $19,600 pesos in the border region.

One of the most important drivers of employment and economic growth in the border region is the maquiladora industry. Since the implementation of NAFTA, the annual rate of employment growth in this industry in the border region rose to approximately 12.1% from 1994 to 1998 from approximately 5.9% in the five years before. At the same time, investment rose from US$0.895 billion in 1994 to US$2.778 billion in 1999 (Salas 2001). The principal reason for the rapid growth of the number and size of maquiladoras was not the provisions of NAFTA, but the impact of the 1994 devaluation of the peso (Gruben and Kiser 2001).[16] From December of 1994 to July of 1995, the peso lost over half of its value in dollar terms. This, of course, dramatically reduced the dollar cost of labor to the maquiladoras and kicked off a spurt of growth that lasted into 2000. This growth was also enhanced by the booming U.S economy and the perception that NAFTA lowered the political risks of investment in Mexico.

Although employment in the maquiladora sector has grown rapidly,

66.3% of the economically active population in the border region is employed in the tertiary (services) sector, followed by 27.6% employment in the secondary or industrial/manufacturing sector. Employment in the primary or agricultural sector is minimal at 4.6%. Important differences exist among the border municipalities. In Baja California, the proportion of employment in both agriculture and industry is two times higher than in Coahuila; the proportion employed in services in Chihuahua is higher than in Tamaulipas and Sonora. The proportion of employment in industry in Nuevo León is higher than the level found for the border region as a whole.

A singular feature of the Mexican border economy is border transactions.[17] Border transactions include income from foreigners' purchases of goods and services in the Mexican border region and these have tended to exceed Mexican purchases (outlays) in the United States. In recent years, this surplus in favor of Mexico has grown significantly. Until 1993, border transaction income had increased at a rate only slightly lower than outlays, yet between 1994 and 1999, the rate of income growth was 2.8% while the rate of growth of outlays was only 0.5%.[18] Consequently, the credit balance (surplus) of US$2.7 billion achieved in 1999 (the difference between an income of US$7.2 billion and an outlay of US$4.5 billion) represented an average annual increase of 20% over the favorable balance of US$606 million for Mexico achieved in 1993 (Banco de México 2000). Thus, the favorable balance of border transactions improved for the Mexican border economy in the NAFTA era.

The varying rates in the increase of income and outlay are reflected in what is called the retention coefficient of border transactions receipts.[19] Between 1986 and 1988, the yearly average of this coefficient was 27%, dropping to 5% during the 1989–1993 period. However, between 1994 and 1999, it rose dramatically to a yearly average of 41%. The increase in the proportion of dollars retained apparently resulted from the changed peso-dollar relationship after the December 1994 crisis as well as NAFTA provisions allowing U.S. goods to be sold in U.S.-style shopping malls throughout Mexico's northern states, thereby reducing Mexican retail spending in U.S. border communities.[20] In addition, since NAFTA was enacted, Mexican customs inspectors began enforcing limits on the value of retail purchases that Mexicans could bring into the country without paying duty. Free trade has not meant free trade for consumers in border communities.

A Shift-Share Analysis of Employment Change: 1985–1997

To provide a more detailed view of the nature of employment change in the border region over this period, a comprehensive shift-share analysis was conducted for all 25 of the U.S. border counties, as well as the six Mexican border states. Shift-share is used to separate employment change over a given period in a regional economy into three components:

1. National component: the amount of employment change that would have occurred in the region if employment in each regional industry grew at the same rate as total employment in the national economy.
2. Industry mix component: the amount of employment change in the region due to a concentration of industries that grew at a different rate at the national level than total national employment.
3. Competitive component: the amount of employment change in the region that is attributable to the regional industry growing at a different rate than the same industry at the national level.

U.S. Results: Border Industry Level

For the United States, three different periods were examined: 1985–1989, 1989–1994, and 1994–1997. Tables 6–8 report the results of the analysis for the entire 25-county U.S. border region. There is clear evidence that the dynamics of border employment have varied over these three periods. The earliest period, 1985–1989, witnessed very rapid expansion of U.S. border employment, with the creation of 383,856 jobs, which amounts to an annual growth rate of 4.1% (see Table 6). During the period immediately preceding the implementation of NAFTA (1989–1994), growth was more moderate, dropping to an annual expansion rate of 1.7% (see Table 7). After the implementation of NAFTA (1994–1997), employment growth increased slightly to an annual rate of 2% (see Table 8).

In each of the three periods, employment growth in the border region exceeded the rate of growth of national employment. However, the forces behind the more rapid growth in the border region do not seem to be constant over time. This can be seen by examining the

Table 6. U.S. Border Employment by Industry: Shift-Share Analysis, 1985–1989

	EMP85	EMP89	CHANGE	NAT	MIX	COMP	Growth Rate (Yr.)
Total	2,180,980	2,564,836	383,856	224,718	5,000	154,137	4.14
Farming	44,801	42,444	-2,357	4,616	-8,106	1,133	-1.34
Agriculture, Forestry, and Fishing	36,104	51,739	15,635	3,720	3,236	8,679	9.41
Mining	13,884	11,378	-2,506	1,431	-4,822	885	-4.85
Construction	124,058	142,737	18,679	12,782	3,090	2,807	3.57
Manufacturing	231,687	249,500	17,813	23,872	-21,311	15,252	1.87
Transportation and Public Utilities	78,110	87,658	9,548	8,048	-1,824	3,324	2.93
Wholesale Trade	76,567	94,707	18,140	7,889	-,787	11,037	5.46
Retail Trade	357,691	435,874	78,183	36,855	6,033	35,295	5.07
Finance, Insurance, and Real Estate	180,348	203,846	23,498	18,582	2,882	2,034	3.11
Services	523,973	672,634	148,661	53,988	47,634	47,039	6.44
Federal Civilian Government	79,424	83,132	3,708	8,183	-4,805	330	1.15
Federal Military Government	187,402	195,947	8,545	19,309	-14,941	4,177	1.12
State Government	55,753	62,152	6,399	5,745	-371	1,025	2.75
Local and County Government	191,178	231,088	39,910	19,698	-906	21,117	4.85

Sources: Calculations for the U.S. Shift-Share Analyses (Tables 6–11) were made by Sergio Rey with data taken from U.S. Department of Commerce (n.d.).

changing roles of the industry mix effect (MIX) and the competitive effect (COMP) in Tables 6–8. The mix effect is positive in the first period (1985–1989), but turns negative for the border economy in the second two periods surrounding NAFTA implementation. This implies that, since 1989, the U.S. border region has become increasingly specialized in industries that have displayed below average growth rates in the national economy. Key examples of this are manufacturing and wholesale trade.

At the same time, the competitive effect is positive in each of the three periods for the combined industries in the U.S. border region. This means the growth of the competitive industries (those growing faster in the region than in the nation) more than compensates for any poorly performing industries in the region in all three periods. It is important to note in this regard that the manufacturing sector lost jobs in each of the periods in the national economy (i.e., negative mix

Table 7. U.S. Border Employment by Industry: Shift-Share Analysis, 1989–1994

	EMP89	EMP94	CHANGE	NAT	MIX	COMP	Growth Rate (Yr.)
Total	2,564,836	2,794,495	229,659	211,149	-20,272	38,782	1.73
Farming	42,444	42,696	252	3,494	-6,310	3,067	0.12
Agriculture, Forestry, and Fishing	51,739	61,441	9,702	4,259	12,592	-7,149	3.50
Mining	11,378	11,886	508	937	-2,292	1,864	0.88
Construction	142,737	137,634	-5,103	11,751	-4,765	-12,088	-0.73
Manufacturing	249,500	246,570	-2,930	20,540	-30,168	6,698	-0.24
Transportation and Public Utilities	87,658	108,100	20,442	7,216	2,632	10,593	4.28
Wholesale Trade	94,707	103,267	8,560	7,797	-4,291	5,054	1.75
Retail Trade	435,874	484,432	48,558	35,883	11,973	702	2.13
Finance, Insurance, and Real Estate	203,846	188,668	-15,178	16,782	-19,840	-12,120	-1.54
Services	672,634	825,725	153,091	55,374	80,788	16,929	4.19
Federal Civilian Government	83,132	81,222	-1,910	6,844	-11,734	2,980	-0.46
Federal Military Government	195,947	152,640	-43,307	16,131	-56,297	-3,141	-4.87
State Government	62,152	77,467	15,315	5,117	1,742	8,456	4.50
Local and County Government	231,088	272,747	41,659	19,024	5,698	16,936	3.37

effect). However, in the border region, the manufacturing sector actually added jobs in the first and third periods. While the region did lose manufacturing jobs in the second period, the rate of decline was slower than that realized in the national economy, as reflected in the positive competitive share.

In terms of the major engines of employment growth in the border, both services and retail trade have accounted for the largest (first and second, respectively) sources of job growth in each of the three periods. Moreover, this share has increased since NAFTA's implementation, as these two sectors combined were responsible for over half of the newly created jobs in the region. The positive effects for these two sectors suggests that their contribution to the border economy is not simply a reflection of developments in the national economy, because these two sectors have outperformed their national counterparts.

Focusing on the two periods immediately surrounding NAFTA,

Table 8. U.S. Border Employment by Industry: Shift-Share Analysis, 1994–1997

	EMP94	EMP97	CHANGE	NAT	MIX	COMP	Growth Rate (Yr.)
Total	2,794,495	2,967,287	172,792	133,282	-5,860	45,370	2.02
Farming	42,696	41,772	-924	2,036	-2,466	-495	-0.73
Agriculture, Forestry, and Fishing	61,441	67,723	6,282	2,930	2,145	1,207	3.30
Mining	11,886	12,879	993	567	-1,721	2,147	2.71
Construction	137,634	154,349	16,715	6,564	6,320	3,831	3.89
Manufacturing	246,570	250,403	3,833	11,760	-9,325	1,398	0.52
Transportation and Public Utilities	108,100	121,799	13,699	5,156	2,028	6,515	4.06
Wholesale Trade	103,267	107,008	3,741	4,925	-1,594	410	1.19
Retail Trade	484,432	508,558	24,126	23,105	-508	1,529	1.63
Finance, Insurance, and Real Estate	188,668	203,902	15,234	8,998	2,737	3,499	2.62
Services	825,725	905,357	79,632	39,382	24,321	15,929	3.12
Federal Civilian Government	81,222	80,619	-603	3,874	-8,295	3,818	-0.25
Federal Military Government	152,640	143,270	-9,370	7,280	-11,995	-4,656	-2.09
State Government	77,467	83,424	5,957	3,695	-3,254	5,517	2.50
Local and County Government	272,747	286,224	13,477	13,009	-4,253	4,722	1.62

there are several interesting findings. In the 1989–1994 period, there were four regional industries displaying negative competitive effects: agriculture, forestry, fishing; construction; finance, insurance, and real estate; and federal military government. Yet, all of these sectors, with the exception of federal military government, displayed positive competitive effects during the 1994–1997 period. By way of contrast, Farming displayed positive competitive effects prior to NAFTA, but the effect turned negative in the more recent period.

U.S. Results: Border County Level

Tables 9–11 report the three components of employment change for the 25 U.S. counties over the three periods. These tables illustrate that the aggregate patterns for the entire U.S. border region, reported previously, actually mask a great deal of variation in the growth dynamics of the individual counties. For example, during the 1985–1989 period, employment in the border region grew at a 4.1% annual growth rate. Employment in Santa Cruz County, Arizona, expanded at an annual rate of 7.7%, while at the other end of the spectrum, employment in Dimmit County, Texas, declined by 3.3% annually. Similar findings hold for the last two periods as well, suggesting that border employment growth has not been a uniform process for the individual counties.

Focusing on the pre– and post–NAFTA comparison, Tables 10 and

Table 9. U.S. Border County Employment: Shift-Share Analysis, 1985–1989

	EMP85	EMP89	CHANGE	NAT	MIX	COMP	Growth Rate (Yr.)
Border Total	2,180,982	2,564,835	383,853	224,718	5,000	154,137	4.14
San Diego	1,172,684	1,417,145	244,461	120,828	4,398	119,235	4.85
Imperial	41,330	52,906	11,576	4,258	-225	7,542	6.37
Yuma	41,367	51,042	9,675	4,262	-278	5,691	5.39
Pima	294,415	324,717	30,302	30,335	3,759	-3,792	2.48
Santa Cruz	10,056	13,551	3,495	1,036	63	2,396	7.74
Cochise	37,280	40,642	3,362	3,841	-636	157	2.18
Hildalgo	2,606	3,007	401	269	-63	195	3.64
Luna	5,380	6,267	887	554	7	325	3.89
Doña Ana	48,904	57,847	8,943	5,039	63	3,841	4.29
El Paso	234,215	266,313	32,098	24,132	-1,077	9,043	3.26
Hudspeth	1,187	1,142	-45	122	-65	-101	-0.96
Culberson	1,851	1,765	-86	191	32	-309	-1.18
Jeff Davis	834	955	121	86	-23	59	3.44
Presidio	1,946	1,991	45	201	-41	-114	0.57
Brewster	4,023	3,971	-52	415	6	-472	-0.32
Terrel	789	827	38	81	-29	-13	1.18
Val Verde	15,111	15,527	416	1,557	-206	-935	0.68
Kinney	1,022	1,039	17	105	-31	-57	0.41
Maverick	8,412	9,663	1,251	867	-74	458	3.53
Dimmitt	3,830	3,352	-478	395	-218	-655	-3.28
Webb	42,552	50,754	8,202	4,384	-250	4,067	4.51
Zapata	2,452	2,540	88	253	-170	6	0.89
Starr	8,500	10,292	1,792	876	-276	1,192	4.90
Hildalgo	114,327	133,039	18,712	11,780	-382	7,314	3.86
Cameron	85,909	94,541	8,632	8,852	715	-935	2.42

Table 10. U.S. Border County Employment: Shift-Share Analysis, 1989–1994

	EMP89	EMP94	CHANGE	NAT	MIX	COMP	Growth Rate (Yr.)
Border Total	2,564,835	2,794,494	229,659	211,149	-20,272	38,782	1.73
San Diego	1,417,145	1,449,526	32,381	116,666	-24,274	-60,011	0.45
Imperial	52,906	58,786	5,880	4,355	2,360	-835	2.13
Yuma	51,042	59,760	8,718	4,202	206	4,310	3.20
Pima	324,717	378,398	53,681	26,732	4,662	22,287	3.11
Santa Cruz	13,551	14,367	816	1,116	62	-361	1.18
Cochise	40,642	44,468	3,826	3,346	-1,772	2,252	1.82
Hildalgo	3,007	3,158	151	248	-39	-57	0.98
Luna	6,267	8,199	1,932	516	162	1,254	5.52
Doña Ana	57,847	67,126	9,279	4,762	373	4,144	3.02
El Paso	266,313	299,508	33,195	21,924	-4,844	16,115	2.38
Hudspeth	1,142	1,241	99	94	-8	12	1.68
Culberson	1,765	1,366	-399	145	11	-555	-5.00
Jeff Davis	955	1,052	97	79	-2	21	1.95
Presidio	1,991	2,121	130	164	7	-41	1.27
Brewster	3,971	4,401	430	327	53	50	2.08
Terrel	827	675	-152	68	-24	-196	-3.98
Val Verde	15,527	17,236	1,709	1,278	-636	1,067	2.11
Kinney	1,039	1,023	-16	86	-17	-85	-0.31
Maverick	9,663	12,120	2,457	796	34	1,627	4.64
Dimmitt	3,352	3,480	128	276	-27	-121	0.75
Webb	50,754	68,685	17,931	4,178	640	13,112	6.24
Zapata	2,540	3,461	921	209	-46	758	6.38
Starr	10,292	13,570	3,278	847	27	2,403	5.69
Hildalgo	133,039	162,905	29,866	10,952	1,190	17,723	4.13
Cameron	94,541	117,862	23,321	7,783	1,630	13,908	4.51

11 reveal more evidence of different experiences among the border counties. Specifically, there are seven counties that had negative competitive components in the pre–NAFTA era, yet in the period following the implementation of NAFTA (1994–1997), these same counties had positive competitive components. Two counties saw their competitive nature reverse from positive to negative during this period. The majority (14) of the counties maintained positive competitive components in both periods, while two counties, Hidalgo in New Mexico and Terrel in Texas, displayed negative competitive effects both before and after 1994.

The number of counties displaying competitive growth tendencies

Table 11. U.S. Border County Employment: Shift-Share Analysis, 1994–1997

	EMP94	EMP97	CHANGE	NAT	MIX	COMP	Growth Rate (Yr.)
Border Total	2,794,494	2,967,585	173,091	133,282	-5,860	45,370	2.02
San Diego	1,449,526	1,543,307	93,781	69,134	-3,290	27,937	2.11
Imperial	58,786	61,598	2,812	2,804	-25	33	1.57
Yuma	59,760	64,713	4,953	2,850	-167	2,269	2.69
Pima	378,398	401,611	23,213	18,047	1,133	4,033	2.00
Santa Cruz	14,367	15,167	800	685	-28	143	1.82
Cochise	44,468	47,008	2,540	2,121	-714	1,133	1.87
Hildalgo	3,158	3,097	-61	151	-21	-191	-0.65
Luna	8,199	8,802	603	391	-21	233	2.39
Doña Ana	67,126	68,690	1,564	3,202	-341	-1,297	0.77
El Paso	299,508	307,899	8,391	14,285	-1,620	-4,273	0.93
Hudspeth	1,241	1,323	82	59	-19	42	2.16
Culberson	1,366	1,517	151	65	-12	97	3.56
Jeff Davis	1,052	1,232	180	50	-8	137	5.41
Presidio	2,121	2,262	141	101	-24	64	2.17
Brewster	4,401	5,028	627	210	-34	454	4.54
Terrel	675	674	-1	32	-12	-21	-0.05
Val Verde	17,236	18,065	829	822	-216	223	1.58
Kinney	1,023	1,114	91	49	-17	59	2.88
Maverick	12,120	13,144	1,024	578	-71	217	2.74
Dimmitt	3,480	3,648	168	166	-58	60	1.58
Webb	68,685	74,861	6,176	3,276	-162	3,062	2.91
Zapata	3,461	3,722	261	165	-72	168	2.45
Starr	13,570	15,352	1,782	647	-53	1,188	4.20
Hildalgo	162,905	179,599	16,694	7,770	-91	9,016	3.31
Cameron	117,862	124,152	6,290	5,621	83	585	1.75

increased from 16 in the pre–NAFTA period to 21 after the agreement's implementation. This is particularly noteworthy as the number of counties having a negative industry mix effect also increased from 11 before NAFTA (1989–1994) to all but Cameron County, Texas, and Pima County, Arizona, in the most recent period (1994–1997). Taken together these indicate that the border counties are, on average, becoming more specialized in industries that are growing relatively slowly or declining at the national level. The positive employment growth of these industries in the border context is clearly distinct from the experience of the larger U.S. economy.

Mexican Results: Border Industry Level

Data availability prohibits a detailed shift-share analysis of the regional economies on the Mexican side of the border. As a result, the focus is limited to manufacturing employment at the state level. Thus, the three periods analyzed on the Mexican side of the border are 1985–1989, 1989–1994, and 1994–1997.

Tables 12–14 summarize the results of the shift-share analysis for manufacturing employment for the Mexican border economy as a single region for these three periods. As was the case for the United States, employment growth in the Mexican border economy was greater in the 1985–1989 period compared to the 1989–1994 period (5.46% versus 5.03%). However, the rate of increase in the third period is much greater in Mexico than was the case for the United States, as the former grew at an annual rate of 21% compared to just over 2% north of the border.

Economic growth rates on the Mexican side of the border have also exceeded those of the economies on the U.S. side of the border. Moreover, the level of manufacturing employment growth by 247,845 new jobs in the Mexican border economy exceeded the level of total employment growth by 229,659 new jobs in the U.S. border economy

Table 12. Mexican Border Employment by Industry: Shift-Share Analysis, 1985–1989

	EMP85	EMP89	CHANGE	NAT	MIX	COMP	Growth Rate (Yr.)
Total	585,452	724,101	138,649	14,472	6,968	127,828	5.46
Food and Drinks	95,022	99,887	4,865	2,349	2,658	83,415	1.26
Textiles	50,314	75,366	25,052	1,244	3,315	10,318	10.63
Wood Products	28,474	32,880	4,406	704	2,206	-2,464	3.66
Paper	20,865	25,936	5,071	516	1,573	-3,188	5.59
Chemistry and Oil	57,014	58,406	1,392	1,409	-12,305	-2,656	0.60
Minerals (nonbasic)	39,363	47,160	7,797	973	3,236	-801	4.62
Basic Metals	47,932	41,167	-6,765	1,185	-8,616	12,987	-3.73
Metallic Products	240,975	333,398	92,423	5,957	13,398	28,073	8.45
Other	5,493	9,901	4,408	136	1,502	2,145	15.87

Source: Calculations for the Mexican Shift-Share Analyses (Tables 12–17) were made by the Departamento de Estudios Económicos at El Colegio de la Frontera Norte (COLEF) with data taken from the following publications: INEGI (1991), (1992), (1994); Banco de Información Sectorial (2001).

Table 13. Mexican Border Employment by Industry: Shift-Share Analysis, 1989–1994

	EMP89	EMP94	CHANGE	NAT	MIX	COMP	Growth Rate (Yr.)
Total	724,101	971,946	247,845	-1,233	49,525	199,553	5.03
Food and Drinks	99,887	133,466	33,579	-170	-82,401	116,151	4.95
Textiles	75,366	98,735	23,369	-128	22,199	1,299	4.60
Wood Products	32,880	44,688	11,808	-56	7,989	3,875	5.25
Paper	25,936	38,914	12,978	-44	10,310	2,712	7.00
Chemistry and Oil	58,406	81,639	23,233	-99	4,247	19,086	5.74
Minerals (nonbasic)	47,160	58,167	11,007	-80	10,381	706	3.56
Basic Metals	41,167	25,241	-15,926	-70	-16,894	1,038	-7.83
Metallic Products	333,398	478,714	145,316	-568	89,599	56,285	6.21
Other	9,901	12,382	2,481	-17	4,097	-1,599	3.80

Table 14. Mexican Border Employment by Industry: Shift-Share Analysis, 1994–1997

	EMP94	EMP97	CHANGE	NAT	MIX	COMP	Growth Rate (Yr.)
Total	971,946	1,440,262	468,316	418,901	537,145	-487,730	21.73
Food and Drinks	144,766	185,869	41,103	62,393	54,125	-75,415	13.31
Textiles	255,592	325,250	69,658	110,158	173,031	-213,531	12.81
Wood Products	125,521	197,765	72,244	54,099	117,974	-99,829	25.52
Paper	85,381	119,601	34,220	36,799	112,875	-115,454	18.36
Chemistry and Oil	221,593	344,116	122,523	95,505	15,311	11,707	24.62
Minerals (nonbasic)	139,093	267,661	128,568	59,948	63,829	4,791	38.72
Basic Metals	41,167	25,241	-15,926	-70	-16,894	1,038	-21.70
Metallic Products	333,398	478,714	145,316	-568	89,599	56,285	19.83
Other	9,901	12,382	2,481	-17	4,097	-1,599	11.83

during the 1989–1994 period. Between 1994 and 1997, this differential is even more striking as the Mexican manufacturing border economy added more than 468,000 jobs in just two years (see Table 14). This growth has also been somewhat concentrated, as over half of the Mexican manufacturing employment increase was associated with the metallic products sector in the 1989–1994 period. This sector also was responsible for over two-thirds of the manufacturing employment growth during the 1985–1989 period and just under a third of the growth in the latest period.

The robust growth of manufacturing employment in the Mexican border states is also reflected in the competitive components displayed in Tables 12–14. In both of the first two periods, the competitive effect or employment change due to the regional industry growing at a different rate than the national industry is the leading component of employment change for the aggregate manufacturing sector in Mexico's border economy. This is very clear evidence that the dynamic characteristics of the border economy in Mexico were fundamentally distinct from those of the national economy. However, in the last period, the border manufacturing economy had a negative competitive component. This indicates that the growth in manufacturing on the border, while substantial, was actually occurring at a less rapid pace than was the case in the rest of Mexico.

The strong competitive component of employment growth in the Mexican border economy in the first two periods suggests that the nature of the relationship between the border economy and the wider national economy may be very different across the two sides of the border. In the U.S. case, it was the national, not the competitive, component that was the largest element of manufacturing employment growth for the border economies (see Tables 6 and 7). In contrast, the national component became the largest source of employment growth in the Mexican border in the 1994–1997 period. This may reflect the impact of NAFTA for Mexico as a whole. However, the extent to which these shifts are due to NAFTA or reflect other factors remains an area for future research.

Mexican Results: Border State Level

Tables 15–17 provide insight into the regional dimension of border employment dynamics in Mexico. During the three periods, manufacturing employment growth was positive in all six Mexican border states. This stands in contrast to what was found on the U.S. side of the border during the same time periods, where some counties lost jobs in one or more of the periods. While the Mexican border economy added some 247,845 manufacturing jobs from 1989 to 1994 (see Table 16), the U.S. border region experienced a loss of 2,930 manufacturing jobs (see Table 7).

At the same time, all six Mexican states had positive competitive employment shares in both of the earlier periods, although only Chihuaha and Baja California had positive competitive components in the 1994–1997 period. This is also different from the U.S. border experience, where there was a larger mix of counties with positive and negative components. With one exception—Chihuahua in the second peri-

Table 15. Mexican Border Manufacturing Employment by States: Shift-Share Analysis, 1985–1989

	EMP85	EMP89	CHANGE	NAT	MIX	COMP	Growth Rate (Yr.)
Border Total	585,452	724,101	138,649	14,472	6,968	117,209	5.46
Tamaulipas	67,813	98,115	30,302	1,676	-940	29,565	9.67
Nuevo León	196,815	205,221	8,406	4,865	-1,056	4,597	1.05
Coahuila	89,785	108,828	19,043	2,219	-1,691	18,515	4.93
Sonora	51,460	65,249	13,789	1,272	1,531	10,986	6.11
Chihuahua	122,822	168,029	45,207	3,036	6,439	35,731	8.15
Baja California	56,757	78,659	21,902	1,403	2,685	17,814	8.50

Table 16. Mexican Border Manufacturing Employment by States: Shift-Share Analysis, 1989–1994

	EMP89	EMP94	CHANGE	NAT	MIX	COMP	Growth Rate (Yr.)
Border Total	724,101	971,946	247,845	-1,233	49,525	199,553	5.03
Tamaulipas	98,115	144,766	46,651	-167	5,844	40,974	6.70
Nuevo León	205,221	255,592	50,371	-349	11,474	39,246	3.73
Coahuila	108,828	125,521	16,693	-185	-2,572	19,450	2.41
Sonora	65,249	85,381	20,132	-111	-3,226	23,469	4.58
Chihuahua	168,029	221,593	53,564	-286	30,832	23,018	4.72
Baja California	78,659	139,093	60,434	-134	7,173	53,395	9.97

Table 17. Mexican Border Manufacturing Employment by States: Shift-Share Analysis, 1994–1997

	EMP94	EMP97	CHANGE	NAT	MIX	COMP	Growth Rate (Yr.)
Border Total	971,946	1,440,262	468,316	418,901	537,145	-487,730	21.73
Tamaulipas	144,766	185,869	41,103	62,393	54,125	-75,415	13.31
Nuevo León	255,592	325,250	69,658	110,158	173,031	-213,531	12.81
Coahuila	125,521	197,765	72,244	54,099	117,974	-99,829	25.52
Sonora	85,381	119,601	34,220	36,799	112,875	-115,454	18.36
Chihuahua	221,593	344,116	122,523	95,505	15,311	11,707	24.62
Baja California	139,093	267,661	128,568	59,948	63,829	4,791	38.72

od (1989–1994)—the competitive effect is the largest source of employment growth for each region in the first two periods. In the case of Chihuahua, its industrial mix effect was larger than the competitive effect. This was due to its heavy specialization in metallic products, which accounts for over half of its manufacturing employment. In the final period, however, the competitive component was the smallest source of growth in all six of the Mexican border states and is negative in four of these. Again, this reflects the relatively stronger performance of the larger Mexican manufacturing economy.

Although the border manufacturing industries in Mexico grew at a slower rate than their national counterparts in the 1994–1997 period, it is important to compare this growth against that displayed by the U.S. border manufacturing sector. The latter grew at an annual rate of just over 0.5% compared to an annual rate of over 20% on the Mexican side of the border. Clearly, the experiences of both sides of the border have been radically different since the implementation of NAFTA.

IV

Major Findings of the Surveys: Perceptions of Local Stakeholders

The type of data presented in the previous section can provide valuable insight into how the demographic and economic structures have changed compared to their respective national economies during the NAFTA era. Nevertheless, the case can be made that such data provide only one dimension of the changes that have occurred and that other analytical techniques are needed, including econometric analysis and/or direct surveys. The NOBE/REF research team decided to conduct a survey of local experts and community leaders (local stakeholders) in each large community on both sides of the border to ascertain their sense of how their own community has changed since the implementation of NAFTA. Additionally, it was hoped that the survey would provide preliminary information on the factors that were instrumental in bringing about those changes. Finally, the survey was used to identify the types of analytical tools these communities currently have and those they would like to have in order to monitor various aspects of their local economic development situation.

This section reports on the two surveys carried out—one in the United States and one in Mexico—during the summer of 1999. In each case, the sample of respondents surveyed is described and then their responses to various questions regarding the local economy, infrastructure, or environment is reported. Each of the figures (1–36) illustrates responses to key questions that are discussed in the text. It should be noted that the respondents were specifically asked to answer the questions based on their own perceptions. If respondents did not have clear perceptions, they had the option of selecting "no opinion," "unsure," "not sure," or a similar response.

Survey of U.S. Border Communities: Main Findings

Survey Characteristics

A group of local experts and community leaders from the eight largest U.S. border communities were selected based on their status as individuals informed about at least one aspect of their local community, such as the economy, the environment, infrastructure, and quality of life. They were selected from six categories as indicated below. Of the 147 individuals who completed the questionnaires, the respondents were distributed as follows:

National government agency representatives	7	4.8%
State government agency representatives	11	7.5%
Local government agency representatives	33	22.4%
Quasi-government organization representatives*	24	16.3%
Newspapers and academic professionals	35	23.8%
Nongovernmental organization representatives	37	25.2%
Total respondents	147	100.0%

* Quasi-government organizations include groups such as local chambers of commerce and economic development corporations.

With respect to geographical representation, every effort was made to obtain 10 to 15 completed questionnaires in each of the small U.S. border communities and 30 to 40 in the two largest counties, San Diego and El Paso. As can be seen below, however, the final distribution of respondents did not always conform to the original design.

San Diego	36	24.5%
Imperial	12	8.2%
Yuma	19	12.9%
Nogales	9	6.1%
El Paso	33	22.4%
Eagle Pass	3	2.0%
McAllen	10	6.8%
Brownsville	7	4.8%
Laredo	18	12.2%
Total respondents	147	100.0%

In terms of familiarity with the issues probed in the questionnaire, 45% of the respondents had worked in their present positions for less than five years, while 65% had worked in the same organization for five years or longer.

Survey Responses

In the following sections, the responses regarding the main topics included in the questionnaire are summarized. These include NAFTA and non–NAFTA induced impacts on the local economy, local infrastructure, and the local environment, as well as tools for analyzing and monitoring local demographic, economic, and infrastructure conditions. In each case, an overall summary of the survey responses is presented, grouping all localities and all types of respondents, using both figures and explanatory text. Where there is significant agreement among all the localities and/or respondents no further text is provided. However, significant differences are noted in italics at the end of the appropriate section.

The Economy

The responses outlined in Figure 1 clearly indicate that the respondents had generally positive impressions of NAFTA's impact on their own county's economy. Adding the responses of "increased a great deal" and "increased," it is apparent that at least 65% of the respondents perceived that NAFTA had a positive effect on the following: U.S.–based firms moving into Mexico, which could have positive and/or negative effects on the local economy; cross-border cooperation on economic development; firms moving into the county; retail sales; number of jobs available; and the number of higher value-added jobs.

Despite the generally favorable impact of NAFTA, however, only 43% thought that the income levels of people employed in the county had either "increased" or "increased a great deal" during the NAFTA era (1994–1999) while 40% thought that there had been "no effect" and 3% felt that income levels had actually "decreased."

In response to the question, "Apart from NAFTA, what one main factor has favorably impacted the economy of this county during the 1994–1999 period?" there was a wide range of open-ended responses. A large number noted the generally strong national and/or regional economy, while others referred to certain aspects of local development

Figure 1. NAFTA's Impact on County Economy

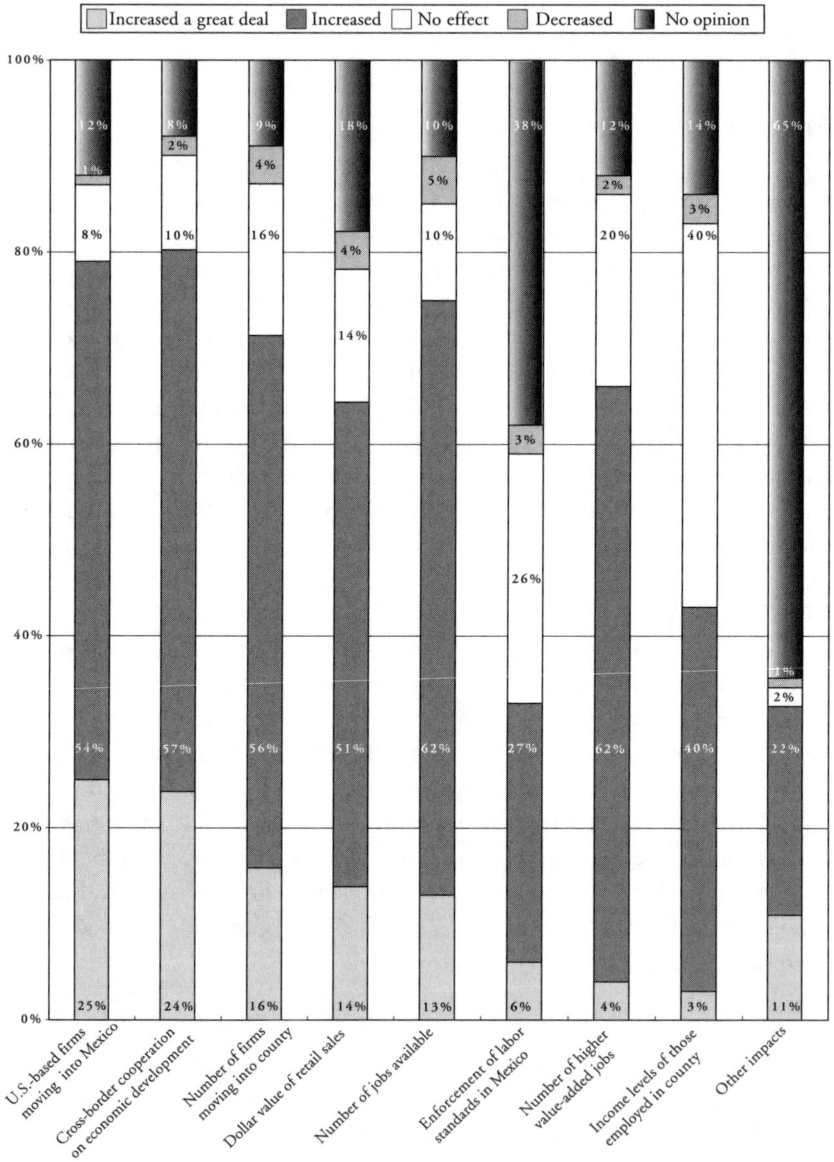

strategies in response to globalization and the new economy, as well as the booming maquiladora industry and the gradually recovering Mexican economy.

Figure 2. Economic Situation in County
1994 to Present (1999)

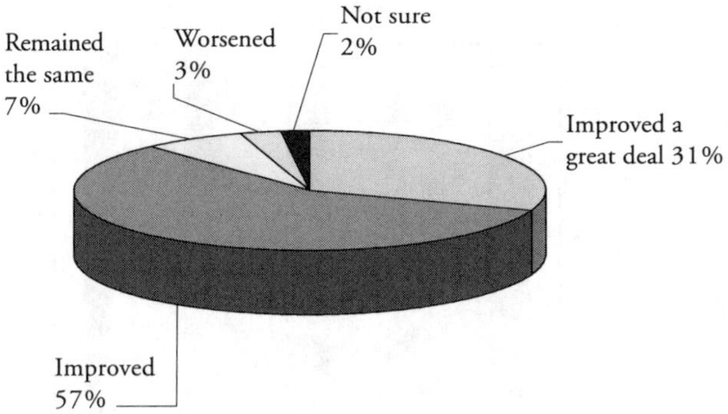

When asked about their perceptions of how the overall economic situation had changed during the 1994–1999 period, 88% thought that it had either "improved a great deal" or "improved," while only 7% thought that it had "remained the same" and even fewer (3%) said that it had "worsened" (see Figure 2).

Infrastructure Issues

Figure 3 clearly shows that stakeholders feel that NAFTA has profoundly affected the infrastructure of U.S. border communities. Again, viewing the volume of responses indicating "increased a great deal" and "increased," it is clear that the respondents felt quite strongly that NAFTA had increased pressures on local infrastructure. Nevertheless, when comparing the overall quality of their county's infrastructure in 1994 with the quality in 1999, 46% of the respondents felt that it had improved, 24% thought that it had remained the same, and only 20% thought it had worsened or worsened a great deal (see Figure 4).

In response to the open-ended question "Apart from NAFTA, what one main factor has favorably impacted the infrastructure of this county during the 1994–1999 period?" most respondents mentioned the strong national and/or regional economy, which led to increased infrastructure funding on more favorable terms.

The question, "Apart from NAFTA, what one main factor has unfavorably impacted the infrastructure of this county during the 1994–1999 period?" evoked two main types of responses. Some

Figure 3. NAFTA's Impact on County Infrastructure

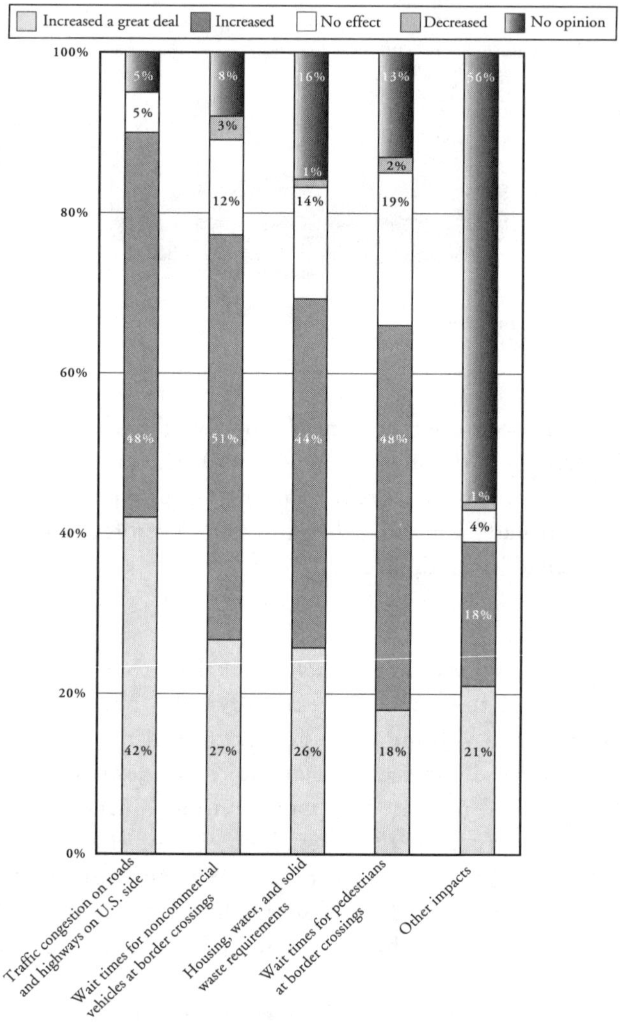

emphasized the expansion of demands on infrastructure due to increased population and traffic flows while others emphasized the lack of an adequate response by appropriate agencies because of inadequate funding, inadequate planning, or poor coordination.

Environmental Issues

Figure 5 clearly shows that the respondents' perceptions of future

Figure 4. Quality of County Infrastructure
1994 to Present (1999)

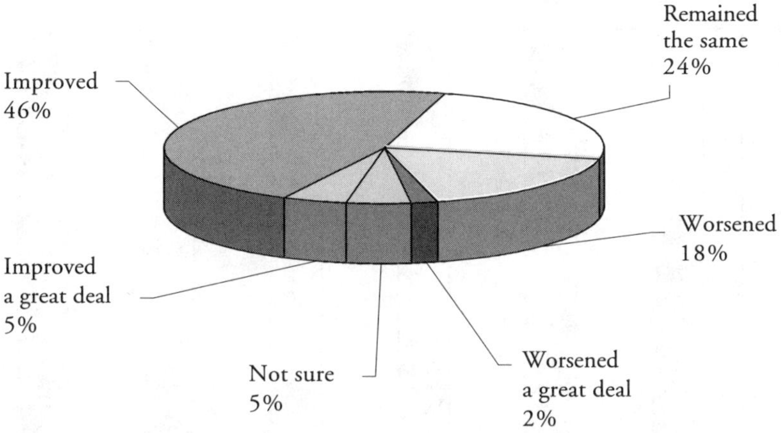

prospects for improving the environment have changed dramatically due to NAFTA. Every question, except the open-ended question asking for "other impacts," evoked a positive response rate of over 60%. Nevertheless, in stark contrast, Figure 6 shows quite clearly that 66% perceived that the actual quality of the environment either remained the same or worsened during the 1994–1999 period, while only 23% felt that it had improved or improved a great deal.

Interestingly, the percent of responses indicating overall improvement in the environment was significantly higher in the smaller communities (29.5%) than in either San Diego (13.9%) or El Paso (18.2%).

Figure 7, which summarizes responses to questions regarding different types of environmental impacts and enforcement patterns, shows widely differing responses. For example, with respect to water quality and water availability on the U.S. side, more than half of the respondents felt that there was no change, while a few felt that conditions had improved and others felt that they had worsened. With respect to local air quality and enforcement standards on the U.S. side, there was considerable disagreement as well.

With respect to air quality, 38.9% of San Diego's respondents noted improvement, while a significantly lower percentage of the respondents in El Paso (18.2%) and the smaller communities (14.1%) acknowledged improvement. Some 31.6% of the respondents in San Diego and 36.3% in El Paso noted improvement of U.S. enforcement standards, while in the smaller communities only 12.8% saw such an improvement.

Figure 5. NAFTA's Impact on County Environment

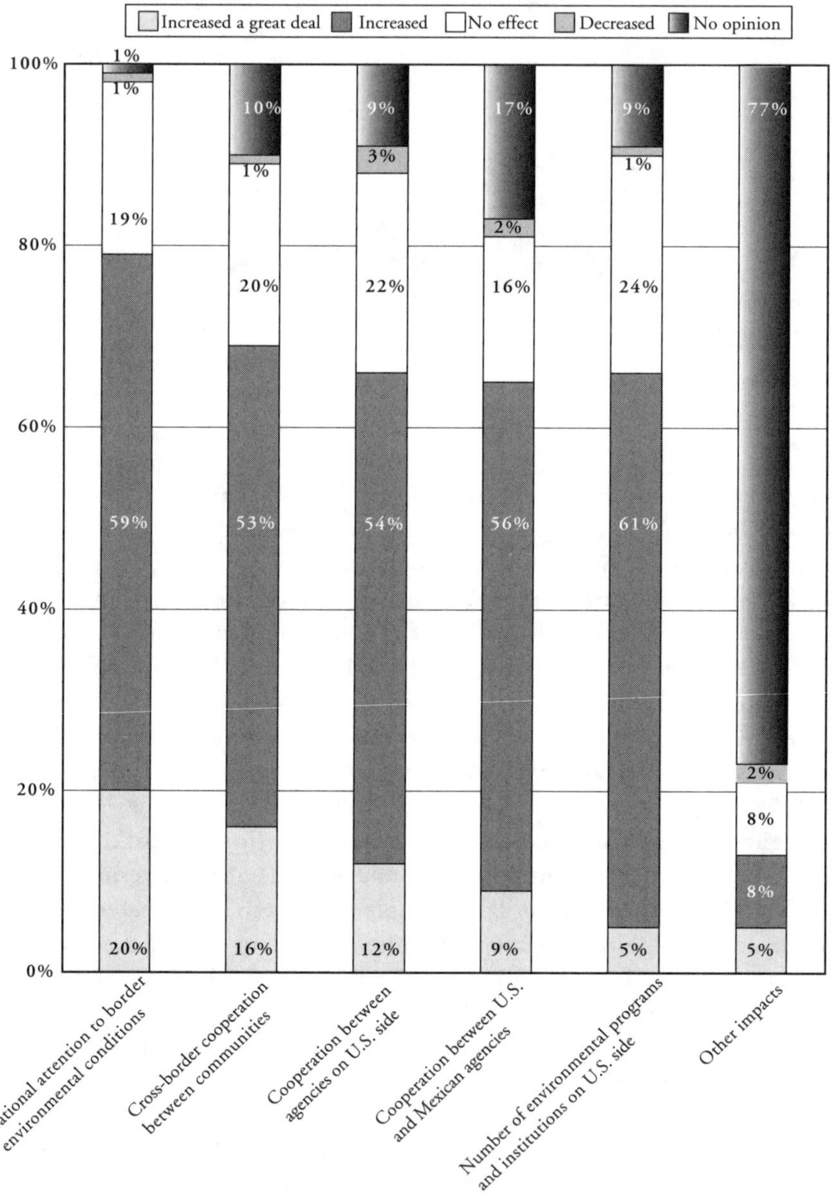

Analytical Tools: Major Findings

Figures 8–18 show the respondents' perceptions in regard to the type of analytical tools and methods they currently use or would like to

Figure 6. Quality of County Environment 1994 to Present (1999)

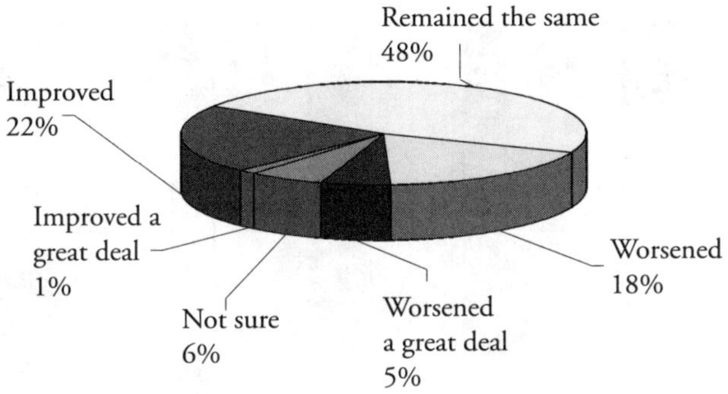

have at their disposal for monitoring and analyzing changing demographic, economic, environmental, and quality-of-life conditions. Since 16 of the respondents did not work for organizations that used or would like to use those analytical tools, the sample size was reduced from 147 to 131. Furthermore, as will be seen shortly, only a small number of those 131 respondents (as few as 19) actually worked for organizations that currently have access to some or all of the tools.

Respondents overwhelmingly indicated that demographic modeling systems to predict population growth and systems for forecasting infrastructure needs are "very important" and "somewhat important." Some 59% regard demographic modeling systems as "very important," while 24% believe they are "somewhat important" (see Figure 8). Some 56% regard systems for forecasting infrastructure needs as "very important," while 25% believe they are "somewhat important" (see Figure 12). Clearly, these two tools are viewed as the most important in all communities. However, there is a great difference between these two systems with respect to access and availability. Fifty-five percent of the respondents indicated that their organizations have access to demographic modeling systems, while only 37% indicated that they have access to systems for forecasting infrastructure needs; some 75% and 80%, with access to these systems, respectively, actually use them (see Figures 8 and 12).

Systems of indicators for monitoring the economy and economic modeling systems for analyzing regional impacts are regarded as quite

Figure 7. Changes in Environment Over Last Five Years

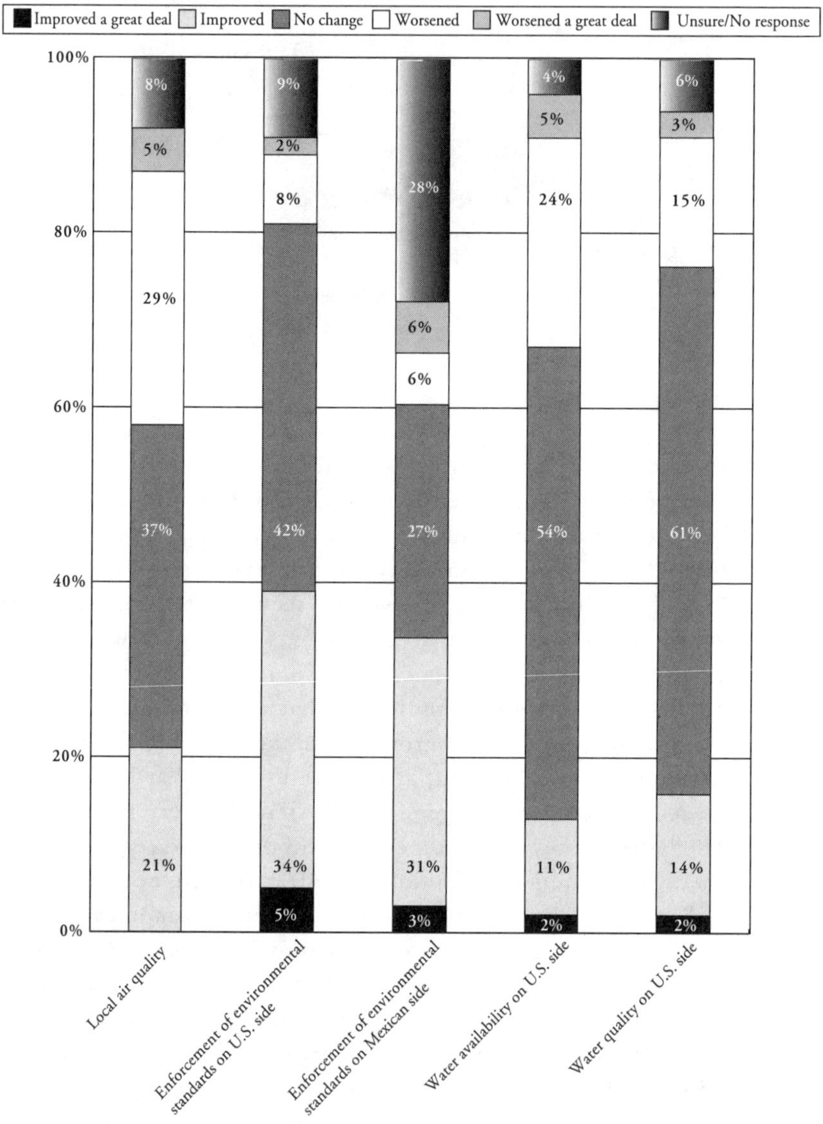

important by the border stakeholders who were interviewed. However, few people have access to them and, in the case of the economic modeling systems, only 58% with access actually use them (see Figures 9 and 10). Systems of indicators for monitoring the quality of life and

Figure 8. Demographic Modeling System for Predicting Population Growth: Importance to Organization (N=131)

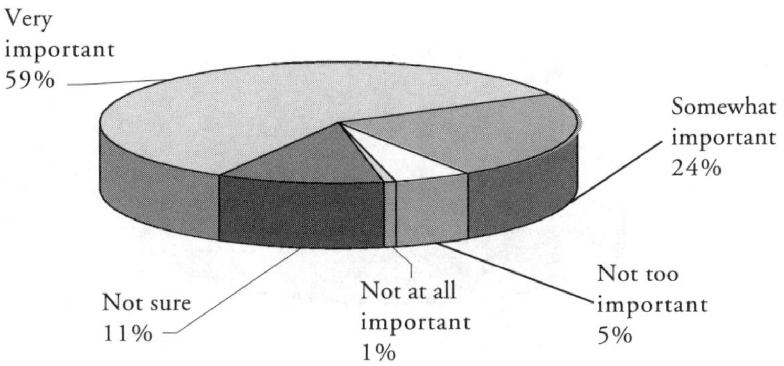

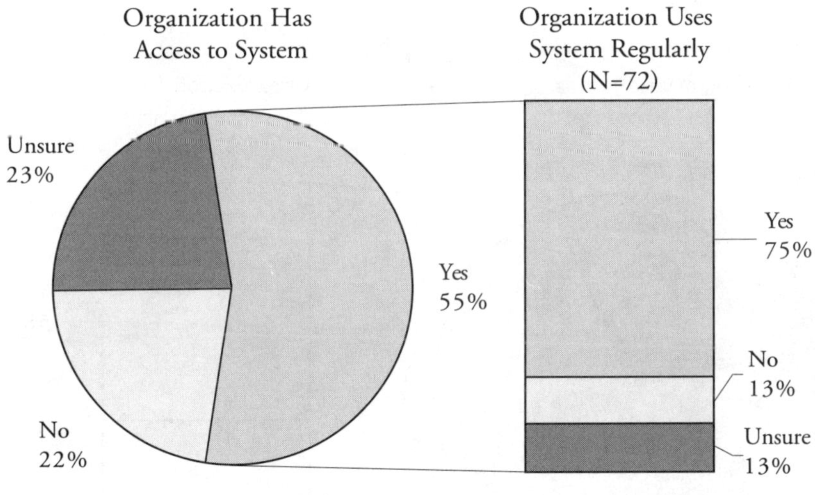

the environment are also important to the respondents. However, the respondents reported very limited access to such systems, with 23% having access to systems of indicators for monitoring quality of life and 27% having access to systems of indicators for monitoring the environment (see Figures 11 and 13). Not surprisingly, San Diego respondents reported having more access to all of these tools than did respondents in the other border communities

Figure 9. Economic Modeling System for Analyzing Regional Impacts: Importance to Organization (N=131)

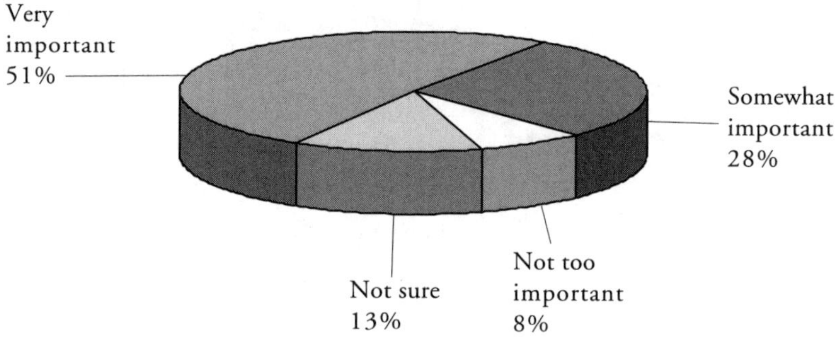

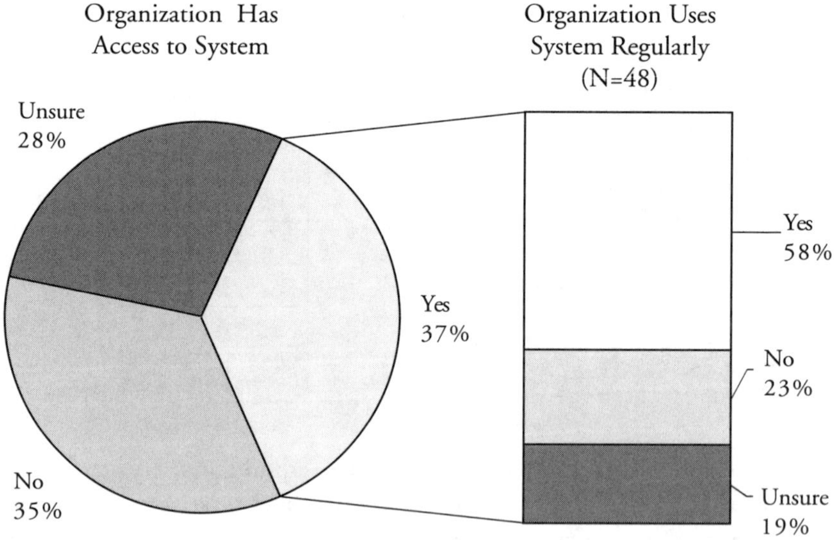

Figure 10. System of Indicators for Monitoring the Economy: Importance to Organization (N=131)

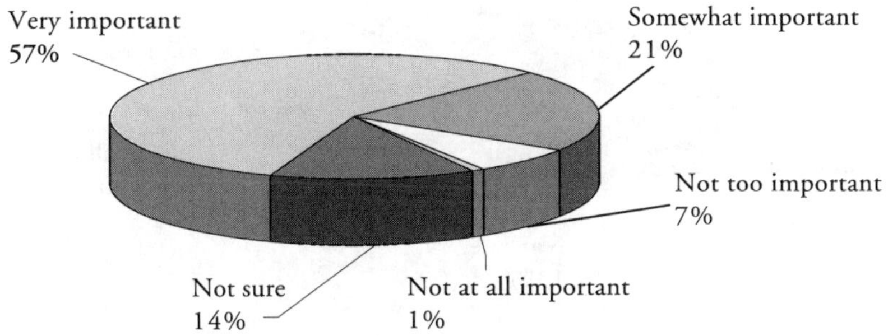

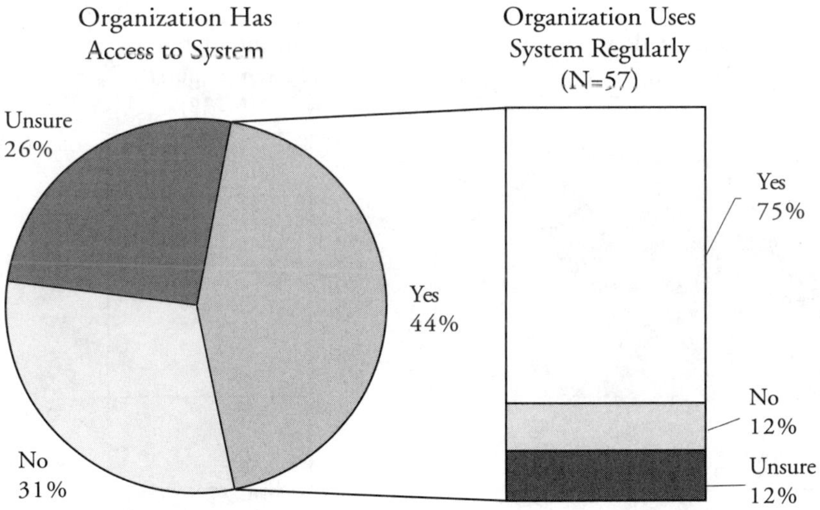

Figure 11. System of Indicators for Monitoring the Environment: Importance to Organization (N=131)

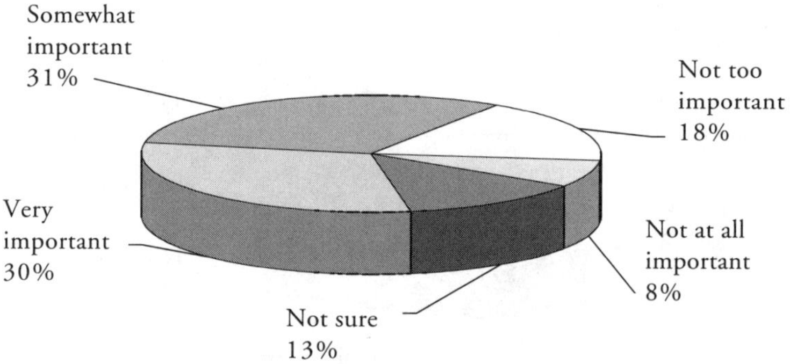

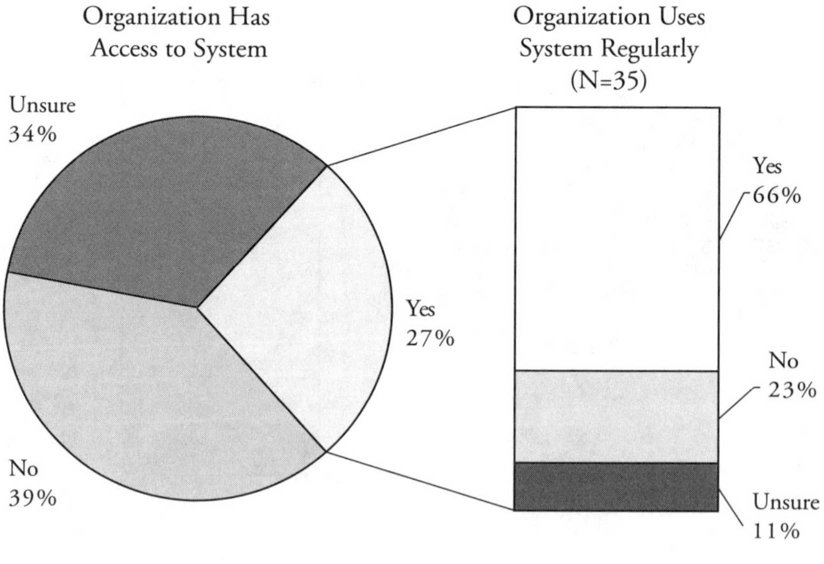

Figure 12. System of Forecasting Infrastructure Needs: Importance to Organization (N=131)

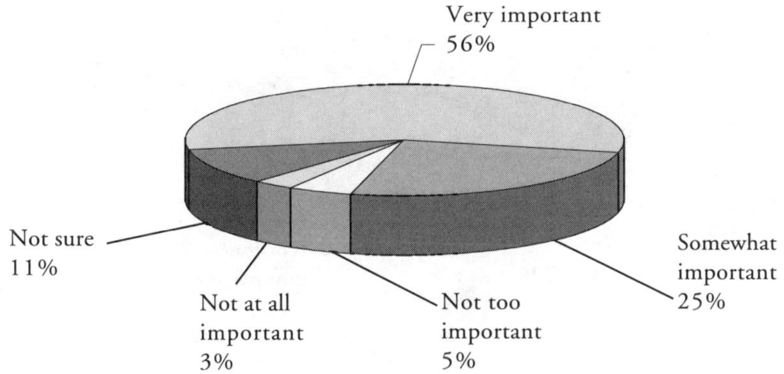

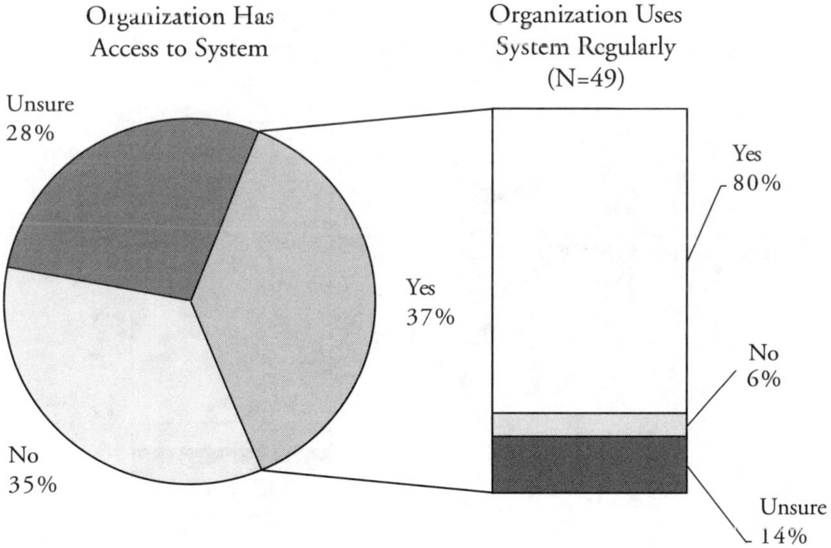

Figure 13. System of Indicators for Monitoring Quality of Life: Importance to Organization (N=131)

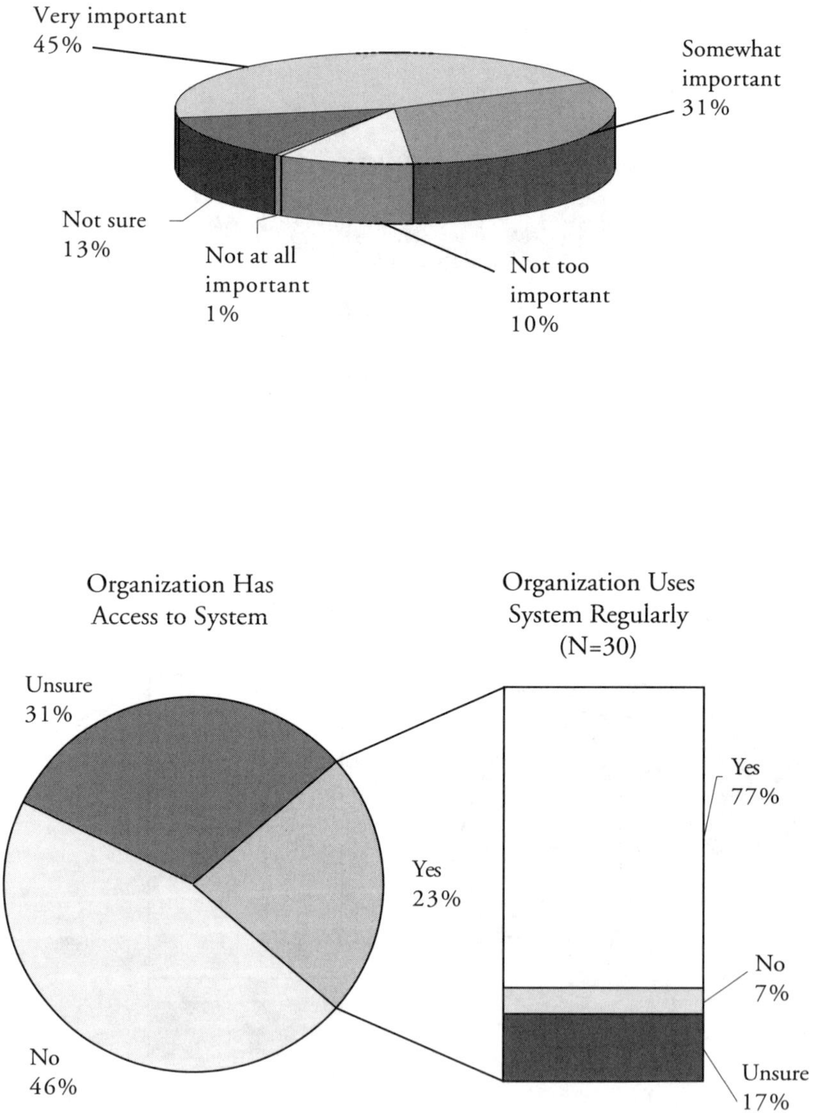

Figure 14. Usefulness of Economic Modeling Applications

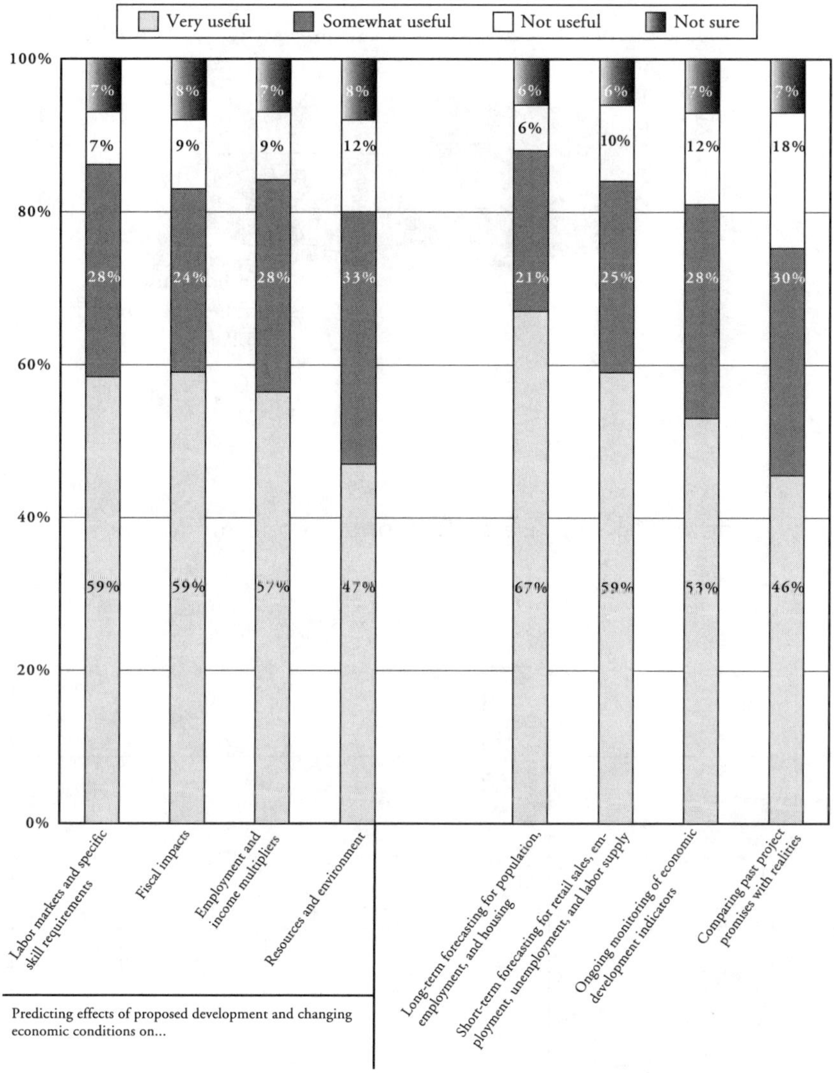

Figure 15. Economic Modeling System Preference

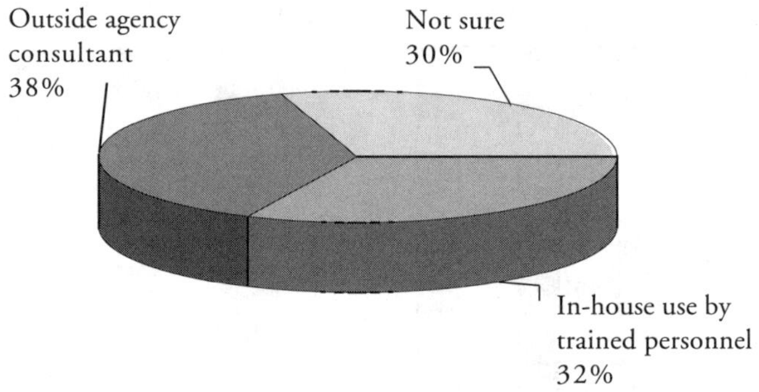

Figure 16. Access to Regional Economic Models

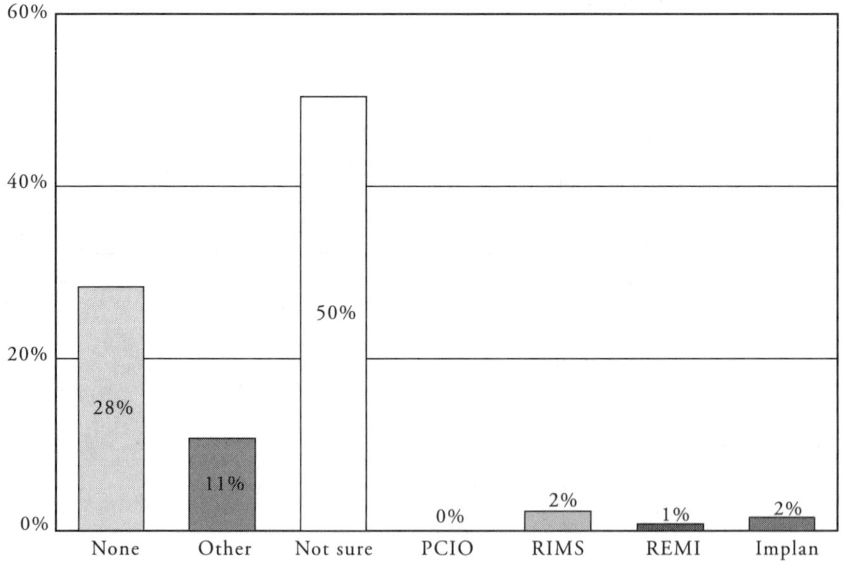

Figure 17. Access to System of Quality-of-Life Indicators

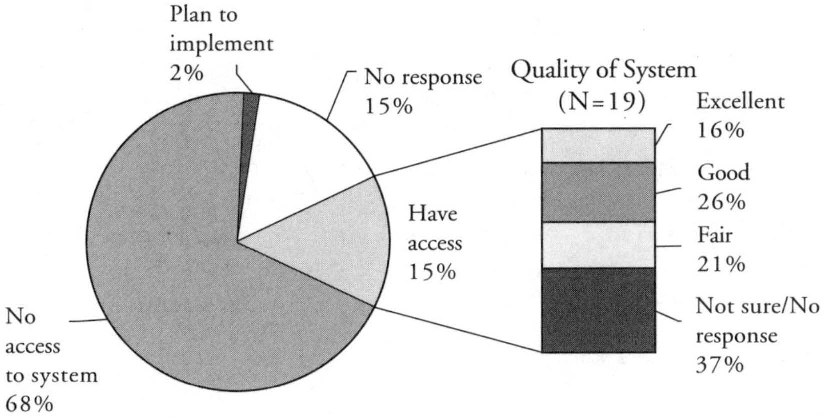

Figure 18. Access to System for Forecasting Infrastructure Needs

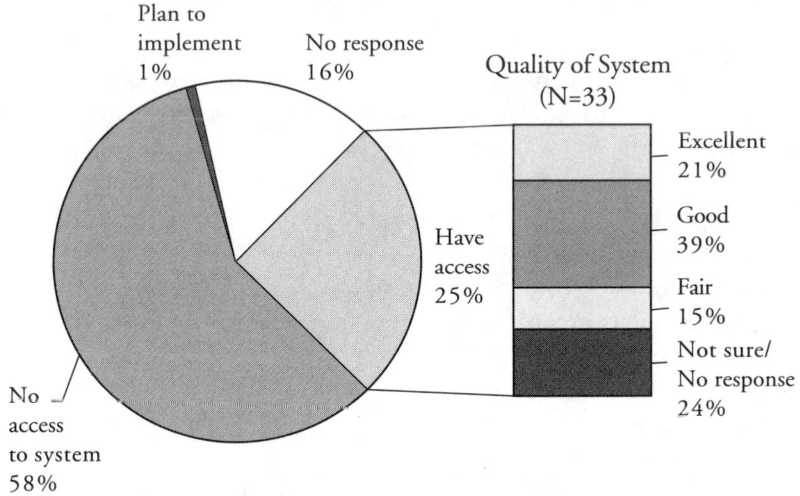

All types of economic modeling applications were regarded as useful, although there were a few that were less useful than others. These include applications for predicting effects on resources and environment, and for comparing past project promises with realities (see Figure 14).

With respect to preferences of the respondents regarding how communities would prefer to gain access to an economic modeling system, there was no clear-cut consensus. Thirty-eight percent indicated that they would prefer to use an outside consultant, 32% preferred to train in-house personnel and 30% were not sure (see Figure 15).

The last section of this report will return to these survey findings and comment on their implications for NOBE/REF and the types of tools that might be most welcomed by local border communities.

Survey of Mexican Border Communities: Main Findings

Survey Characteristics

The same survey conducted in the U.S. border communities was also conducted in the Mexican border communities to measure perceptions by stakeholders. It included a section on NAFTA's impact on economic issues, the environment, and infrastructure; another section on the use of statistical models for projection of economic and demographic variables; and a third that inquired about the quality of life of border residents. In order to provide a range of opinions, participants were recruited from different agencies and sectors. The respondents were distributed in the following six categories:

National government agency representatives	15	10.1%
State government agency representatives	17	11.5%
Local government agency representatives	20	13.5%
Quasi-government organization representatives	39	26.4%
Newspapers and academic professionals	19	12.8%
Nongovernmental organization representatives	38	25.7%
Total respondents	148	100.0%

With respect to geographical representation, the survey was carried out in eight Mexican border cities. The desired number of completed questionnaires for each community varied according to the size and the economic structure of the community. The general rule was 25–30 completed questionnaires for larger cities like Tijuana and Ciudad Juárez, and 10–15 for small communities like Nogales and Piedras Negras.

Tijuana	35	23.6%
Mexicali	23	15.5%
Nogales	15	10.1%
Ciudad Juárez	27	18.2%
Piedras Negras	18	12.2%
Matamoros	20	13.5%
Nuevo Laredo	8	5.4%
San Luis Río Colorado	2	1.4%
Total respondents	148	100.0%

In terms of the respondents' familiarity with the issues probed in the questionnaire, 50% had worked in their present position for five years or longer, while 50% had worked in the same organization for less than five years.

Survey Responses

In this section, the responses of the experts surveyed in Mexico are summarized. The findings are reported in the same format as were the results of the U.S. survey.

The Economy

In response to the question, "How has NAFTA impacted your municipality's economy?" most respondents indicated that NAFTA has had a strong, positive impact on their local economy. The sum of the responses in the categories "increased a great deal" and "increased" indicated that at least 50% of the expert group believed that NAFTA has had a positive impact on the number of available jobs, the number of firms moving into the municipality, cross-border cooperation on economic development, retail sales, and the number of higher value-added jobs in the municipality. However, despite the strong favorable impact of NAFTA, only 38% answered that the income levels of the people employed in their municipality had "increased a great deal" (2%) or "increased" (36%), while 51% thought that there had been "no effect" and 7% felt that income levels had actually "decreased" (see Figure 19).

There was a wide range of responses to the open-ended question,"Apart from NAFTA, what one main factor has favorably impacted the economy of this municipality during the 1994–1999 period?" However, perceptions varied among the municipalities. In Tijuana, tourism and foreign investment were noted. In Laredo, increased import taxes were highlighted. In Matamoros, the booming maquiladora sector and Mexico's monetary stability were identified as

Figure 19. NAFTA's Impact on Municipality's Economy

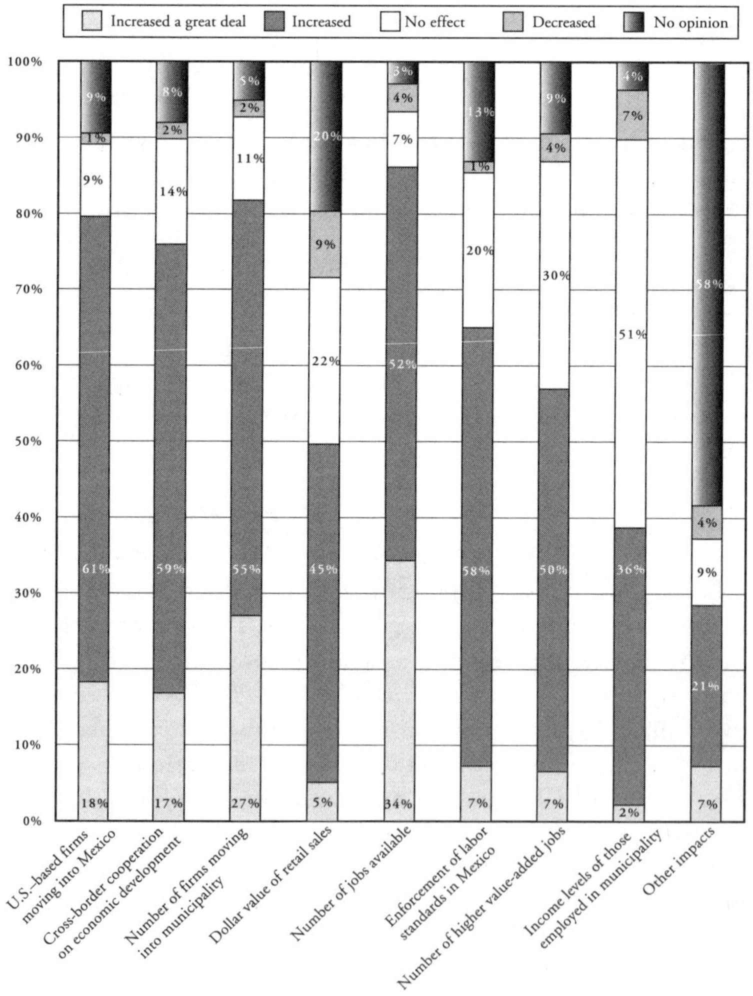

the main factors. In Mexicali, the Partido Acción Nacional (PAN), or National Action Party, was cited as the main factor. In Ciudad Juárez, approximately 20% responded that the maquiladora program was the most important factor. In contrast, the question, "Apart from NAFTA, what one main factor has unfavorably impacted the economy of this municipality during the 1994–1999 period?" produced a unified response from all: internal migration and the lack of water.

When asked about their perceptions of how the overall economic situation had changed during the 1994–1999 period, 83% considered that the economic situation had either "improved a great deal" or "improved," while 10% thought that it had "remained the same." Only 6% said that the economic situation had "worsened" (see Figure 20).

Figure 20. Economic Situation in Municipality 1994 to Present (1999)

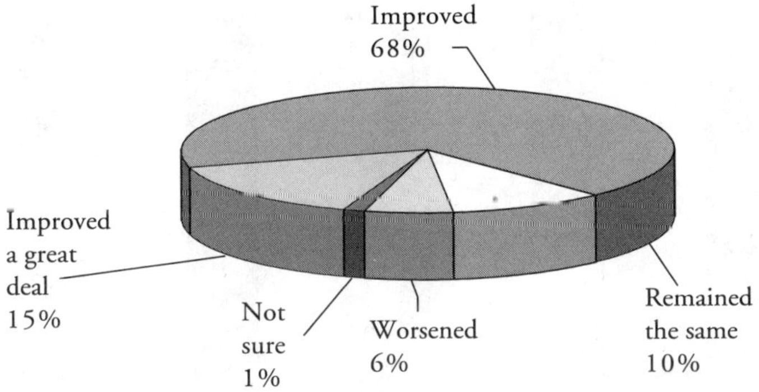

Infrastructure Issues

Figure 21 shows the respondents' perceptions regarding the impact of NAFTA on the infrastructure of Mexico's border communities. In response to the question, "How has NAFTA impacted your community's infrastructure?" almost 90% of the respondents felt that traffic congestion on roads and highways on the Mexican side had "increased a great deal" or "increased." Seventy-five percent of the respondents felt that wait times for noncommercial vehicles at the border crossings "increased a great deal" or "increased." In addition, when comparing the overall quality of their municipality's infrastructure between 1994 and 1999, 77% felt that it had "improved" and/or "improved a great deal,"

Figure 21. NAFTA's Impact on Municipality's Infrastructure

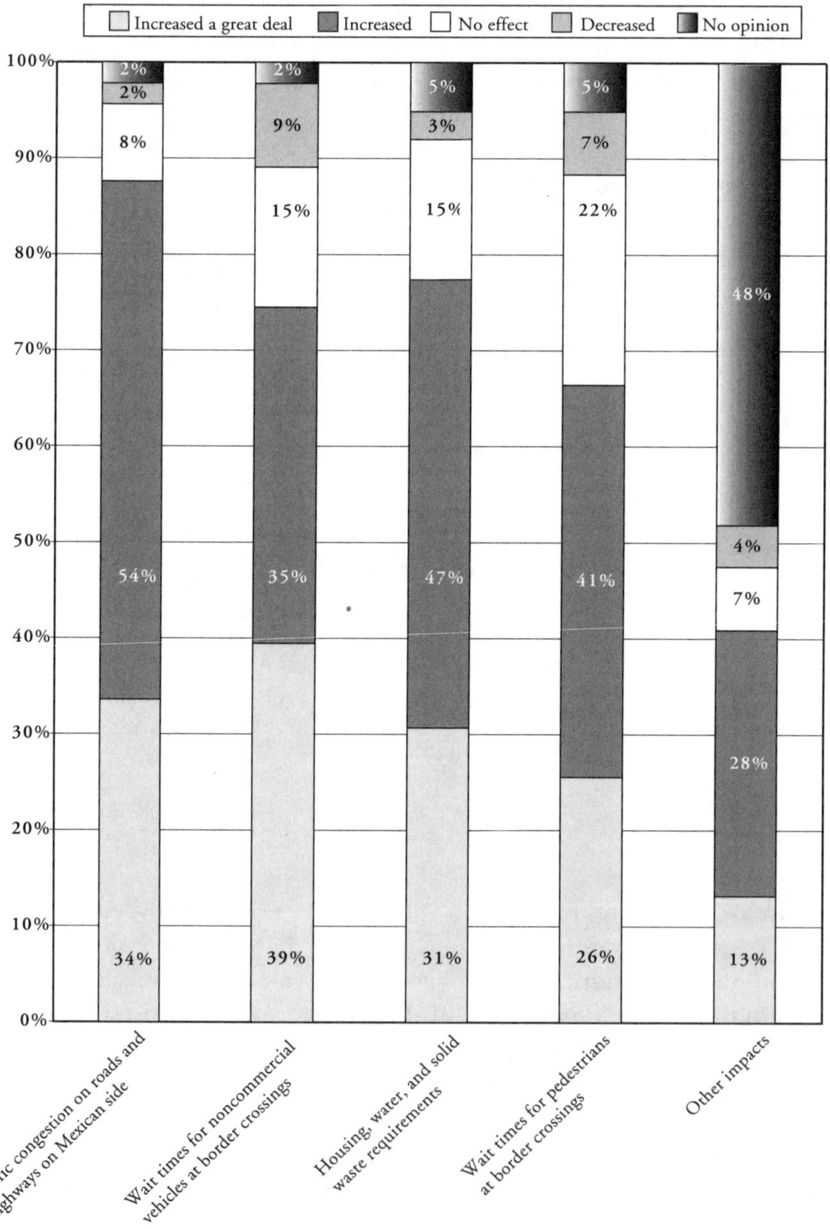

while 12% thought that it had "remained the same" and only 10% thought it had "worsened" or "worsened a great deal" (see Figure 22).

Figure 22. Quality of Municipality's Infrastructure 1994 to Present (1999)

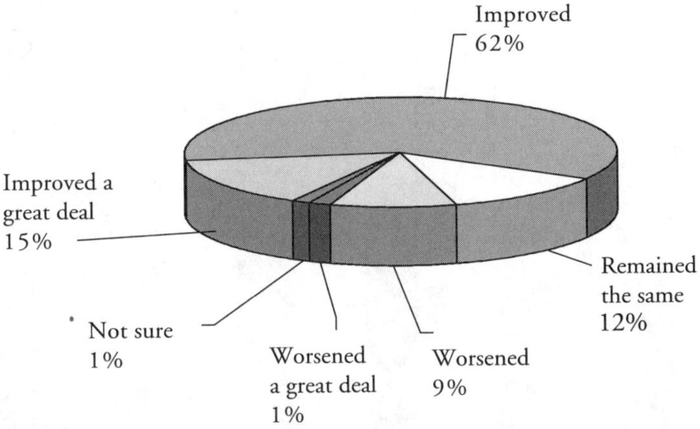

When asked the open-ended question, "Apart of NAFTA, what one main factor has favorably impacted the infrastructure of this municipality during the 1994–1999 period?" there was a wide range of responses, including the construction of toll roads, new international bridges and ports of entry, better urban planning, construction of water facilities, and increased funding on more favorable terms. Most responses to the question, "Apart from NAFTA, what one main factor has unfavorably impacted the infrastructure of this municipality during the 1994–1999 period?" mentioned population growth (migration, increased demand for services, lack of housing, and public security) and inadequate funding and planning.

Environmental Issues

The questionnaire also explored the impact of NAFTA on the environment of the Mexican border communities. Figure 23 shows that the Mexican expert groups' perceptions of future prospects for improving the environment have changed dramatically because of NAFTA. According to the responses in the categories "increased a great deal" and "increased," at least 65% of the expert groups perceived that

Figure 23. NAFTA's Impact on Municipality's Environment

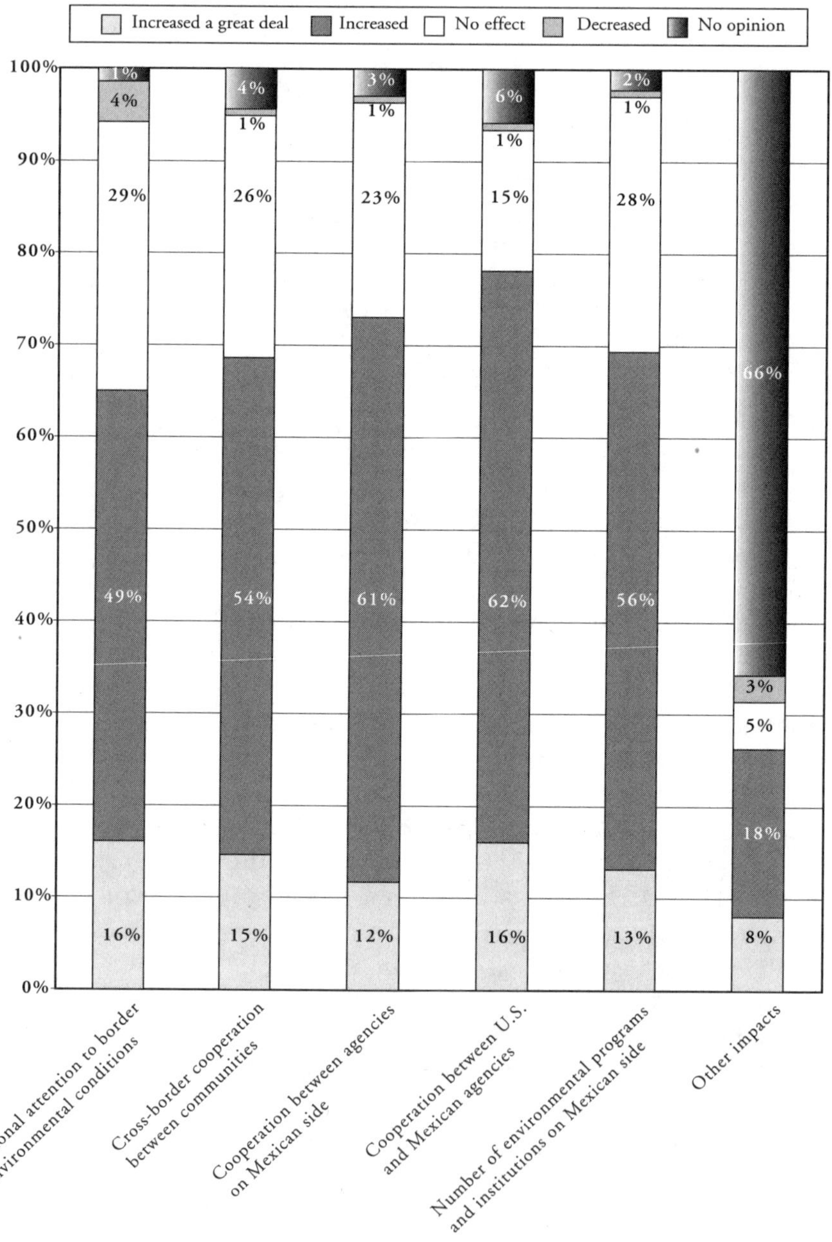

NAFTA had a positive impact on national attention to border environmental conditions; the number of environmental institutions and programs; cooperation among local, state, and national environmental agencies; cooperation between U.S. and Mexican environmental agencies; and cross-border cooperation between local communities.

With respect to the question, "Has the quality of the environment in the municipality changed?" a significant number of the experts in Mexican border cities perceived that the actual quality of the environment either "remained the same" or "worsened" (58%), while only 33% felt that it had "improved a great deal" or "improved" (see Figure 24). In response to the question, "How has your municipality's environment changed over the last five years in terms of local air quality, water availability, water quality, and enforcement of environmental standards on the Mexican side?" every aspect, except for the enforcement of environmental standards, evoked a "no change" or negative response rate of over 70%. The enforcement of environmental standards on the Mexican side shows quite clearly that 42% perceived it had "improved a great deal" or "improved," while only 7% thought it had "worsened" (see Figure 25).

Figure 24. Quality of Municipality's Environment 1994 to Present (1999)

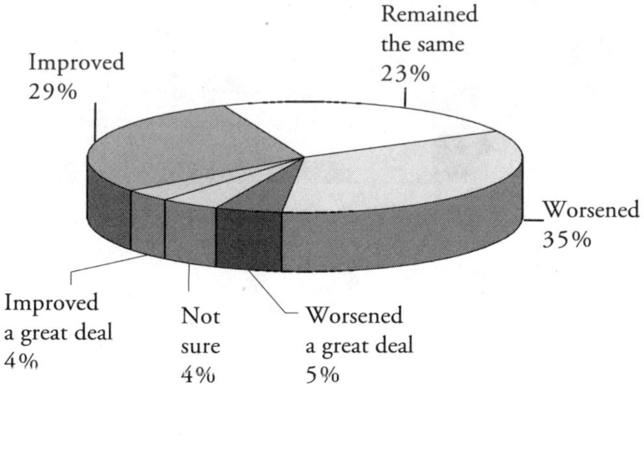

Figure 25. Changes in Environment Over Last Five Years

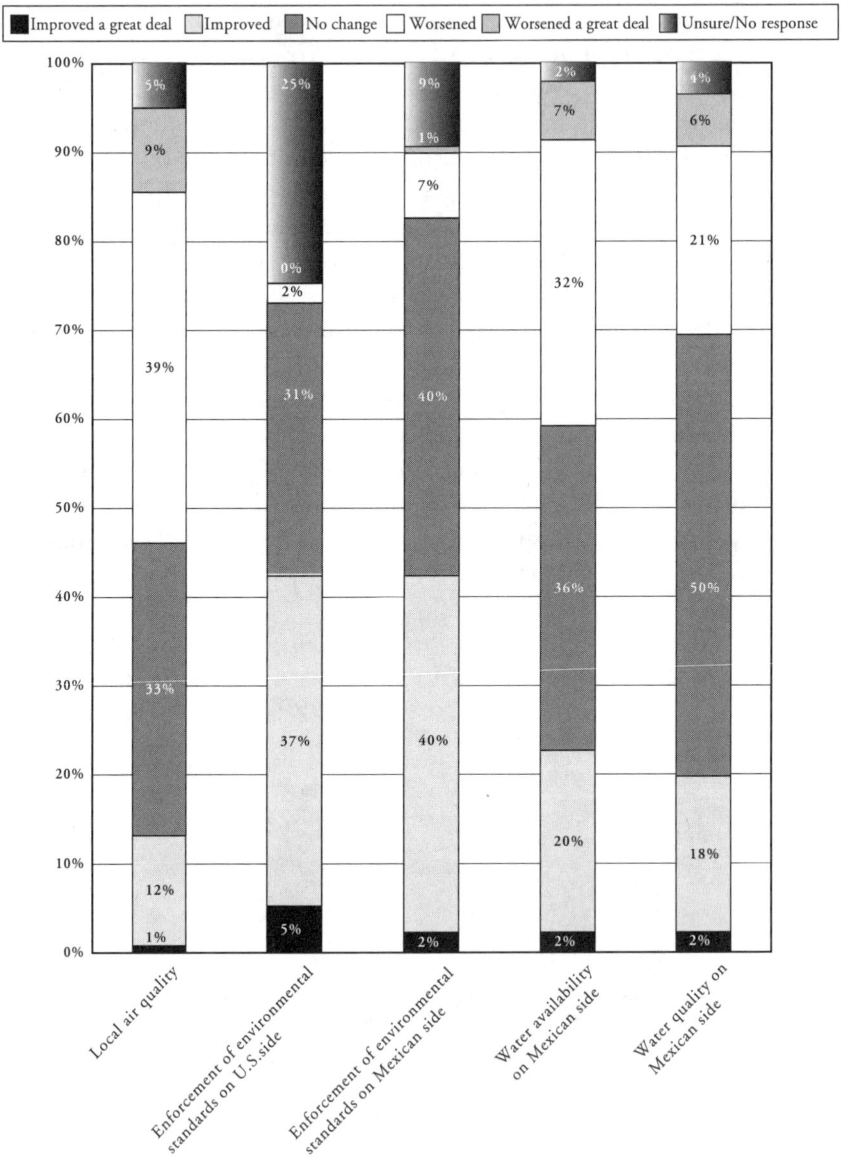

Analytical Tools: Major Findings

Figures 26–36 show the respondents' perceptions with regard to the types of analytical tools and methods they currently use or would like to have at their disposal for monitoring and analyzing changing demographic, economic, environmental, and quality-of-life conditions. Since not all of the respondents work with or use analytical tools, only 97 respondents (65.5%) answered the Analytical Tools section of the questionnaire. When asked what type of analytical tools the respondents would like to have at their disposal, the most important responses were demographic modeling systems and systems for forecasting infrastructure needs. Seventy percent of the participants regard demographic modeling systems as "very important," while 23% believe they are "somewhat important." Sixty-four percent regard systems for forecasting infrastructure needs as "very important," while 34% believe they are "somewhat important."

However, there is a great difference between these two systems with respect to access. Only 18% actually worked for organizations that currently have access to some or all of the tools. Figures 26–36 present the responses to all questions in this section of the questionnaire.

Figure 26. Demographic Modeling System for Predicting Population Growth: Importance to Organization (N=97)

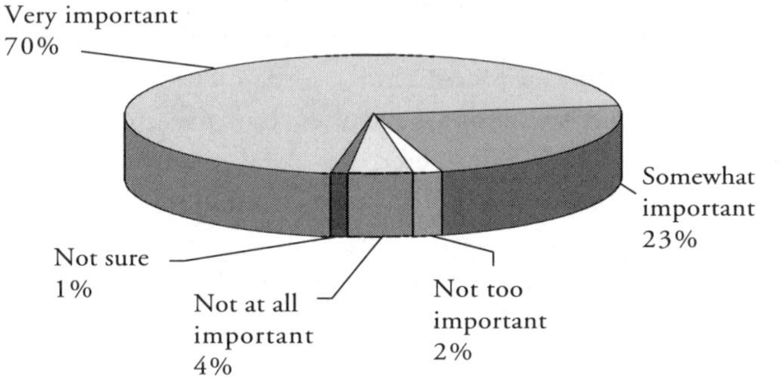

Figure 27. Economic Modeling System for Analyzing Regional Impact: Importance to Organization (N=97)

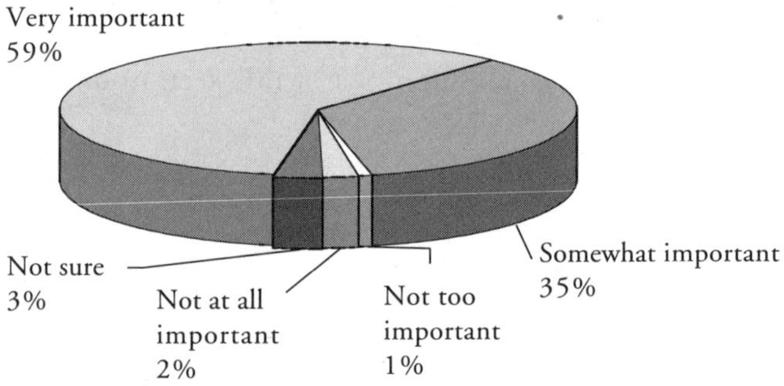

Figure 28. System of Indicators for Monitoring the Economy: Importance to Organization (N=97)

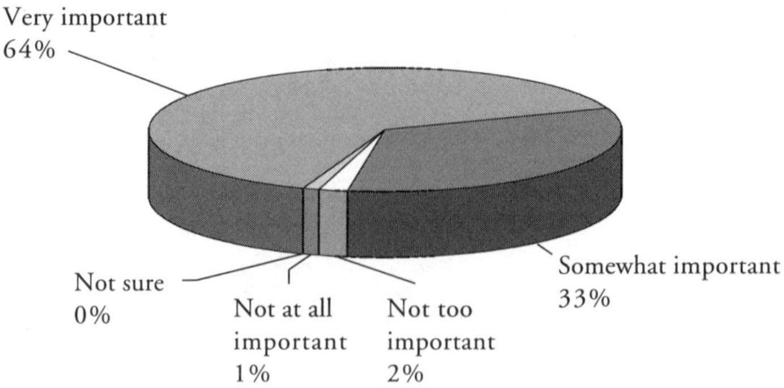

Figure 29. System of Indicators for Monitoring the Environment: Importance to Organization (N=97)

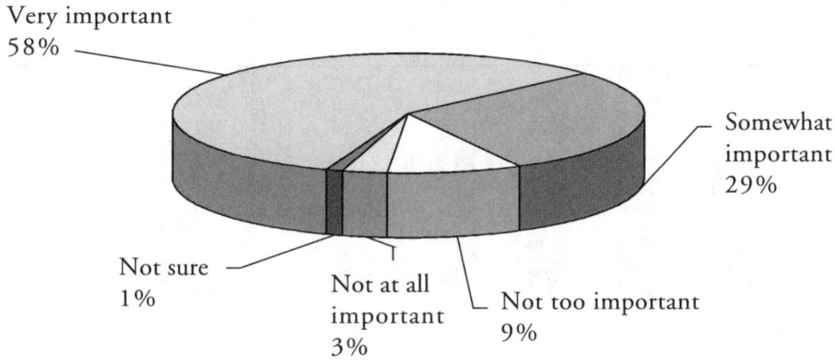

Figure 30. System for Forecasting Infrastructure Needs: Importance to Organization (N=97)

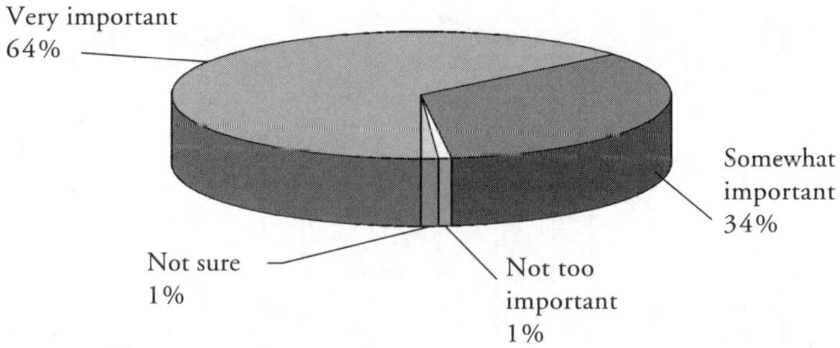

Figure 31. System of Indicators for Monitoring Quality of Life: Importance to Organization (N=97)

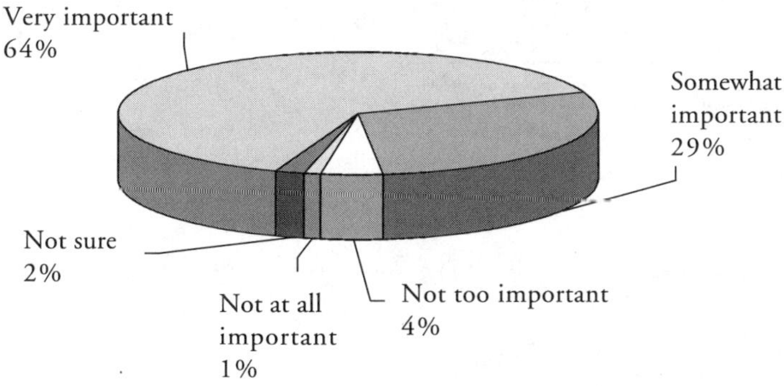

Figure 32. Usefulness of Economic Modeling Applications

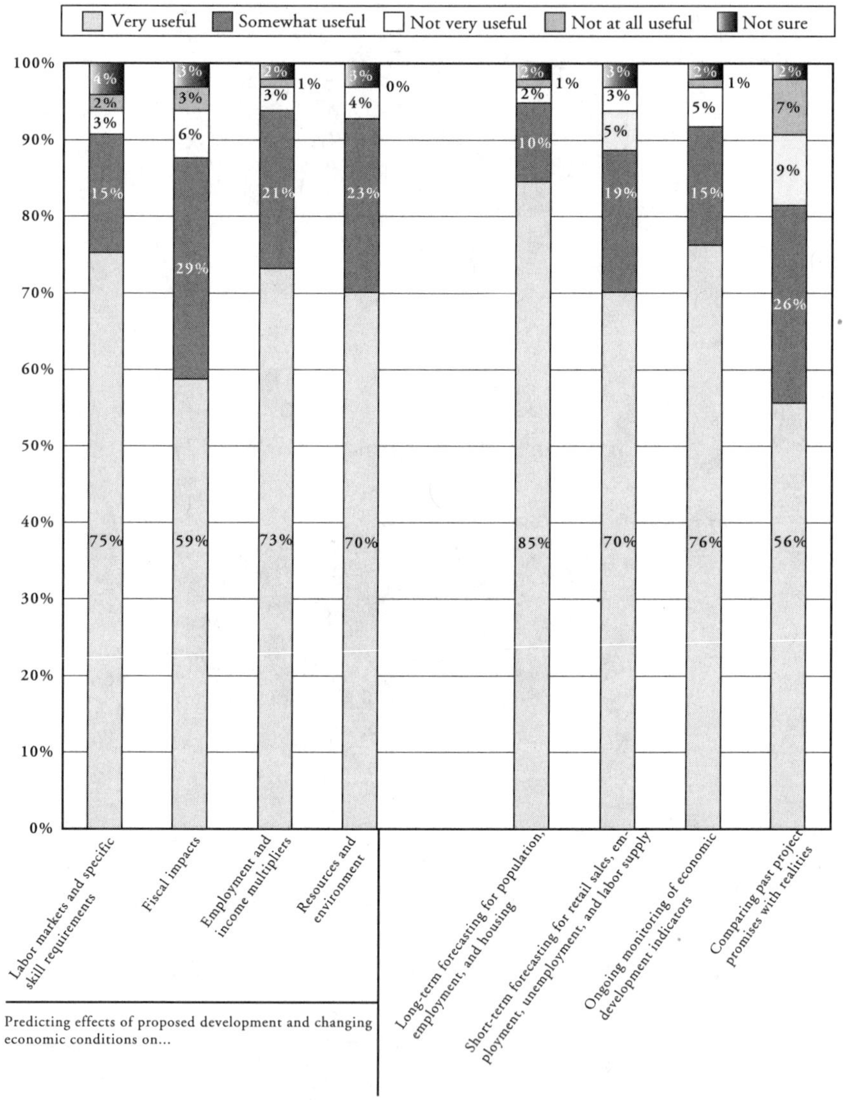

Figure 33. Economic Modeling System Preference

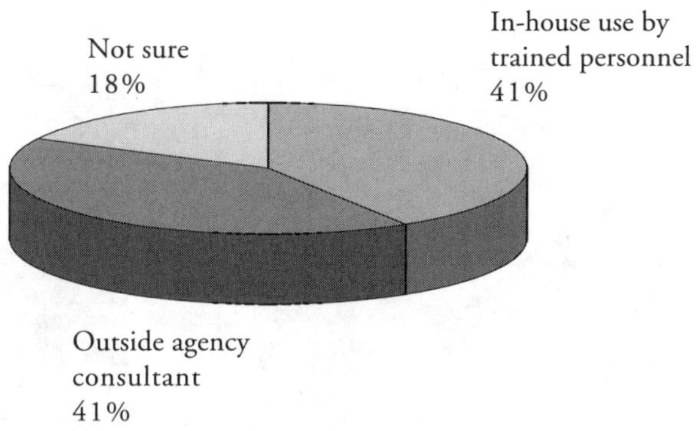

Figure 34. Access to Regional Economic Models (N=48)

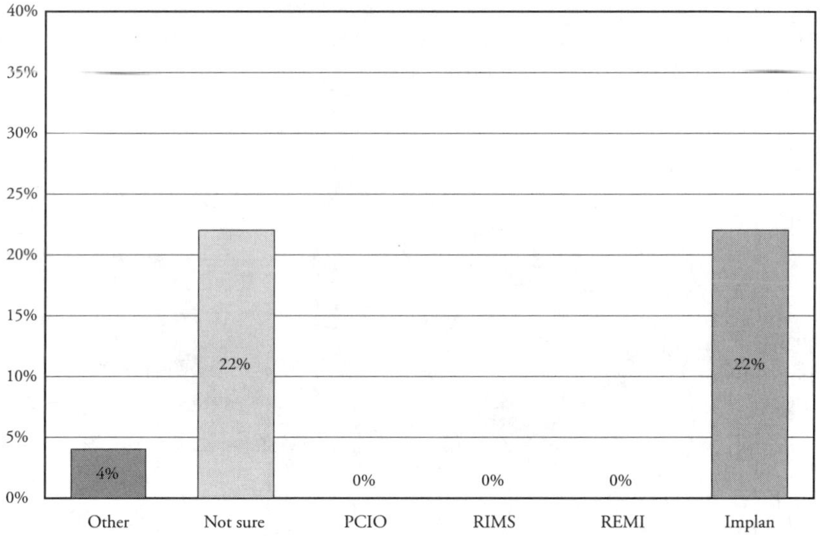

Figure 35. Access to System of Quality-of-Life Indicators (N=137)

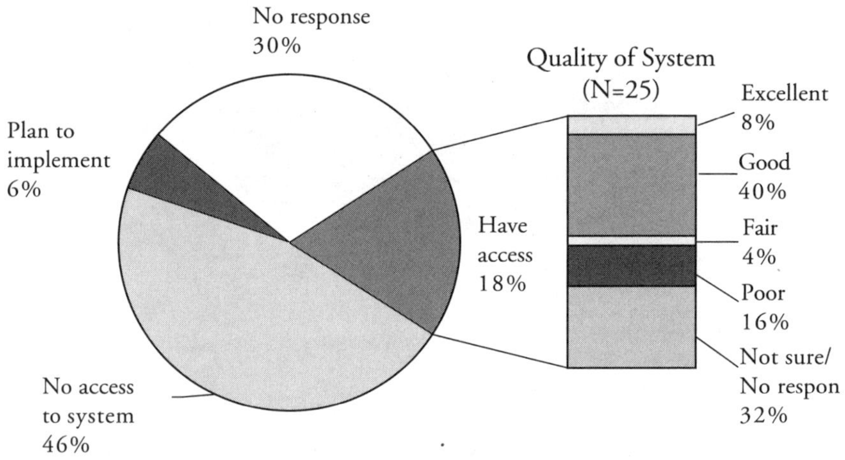

Figure 36. Access to System for Forecasting Infrastructure Needs (N=137)

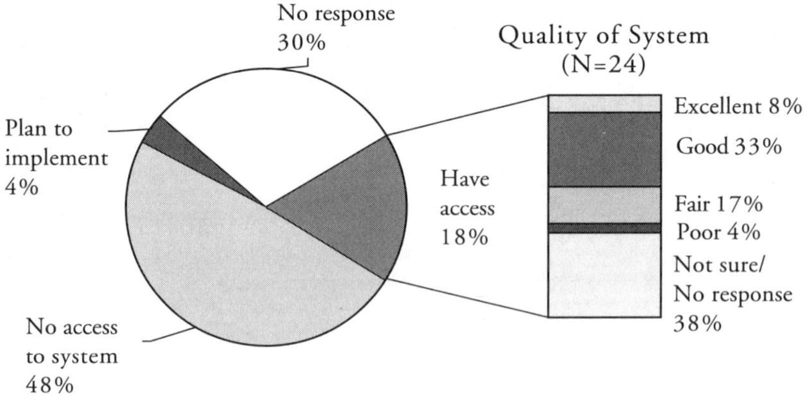

V

Conclusions and Recommendations

Most careful observers of the U.S.–Mexican border situation are well aware that the region's population and economy have expanded rapidly since the implementation of NAFTA. Nevertheless, it is clear that by disaggregating the data into different time periods, different industries, and different subregions, it is possible to better understand the changing structure and performance of this heterogeneous and complex region. Additionally, the surveys of local stakeholders provide further insight into the region's dynamics by tapping into the perceptions of those who are most familiar with the local communities.

In the initial section, a framework for summarizing and discussing the main findings of the study presented in earlier sections is presented. The framework consists of a set of drawn from mainstream economic theory that represent reasonable expectations regarding the likely impact of the increased economic integration that NAFTA has permitted. In the following section, the implications of these conclusions for local, state, and national governments and NOBE/REF as an organization of researchers are discussed.

A Framework for Analyzing the Data

The framework sketched out below consists of seven hypotheses, six regarding the likely demographic and economic impact of NAFTA on U.S.–Mexican border communities and one hypothesis regarding the communities' need for and access to tools of economic analysis. The six economic hypotheses represent the likely impacts that were advanced by the proponents of NAFTA during the ratification process that took place in the early 1990s. In advancing these arguments,

NAFTA proponents drew mainly from mainstream economic theory in terms of how they expected the agreement to impact the U.S.–Mexican border region, a region that was given special consideration and treatment at the time, especially in the side agreements on environmental and labor issues.

New economic integration agreements like NAFTA have always been controversial and all have their proponents and their critics. The mainstream free trade position is drawn from neoclassical economic theory. It is based on certain assumptions about the nature and operation of markets and resource endowments as well as other factors. Therefore, it is subject to criticism on a variety of grounds. Nevertheless, the logic of the agreement itself was largely based on international trade and regional development theory that, in most economists' view, includes the following hypotheses or statements regarding its likely impacts on the U.S.–Mexican border region.[21]

1. Impact on immigration from the interior of Mexico. Given the relatively smaller size of the Mexican economy, NAFTA would have a larger and more positive impact on wages and incomes in Mexico than in the United States. Thus, Mexican jobs and incomes could be expected to rise faster than in the United States, ultimately reducing the pressures on Mexicans to migrate from the interior of the country to its northern border region and into the United States.

2. Impact on the border region's infrastructure, environment, and employment in trade-related sectors. Due to lower tariff and nontariff barriers, NAFTA would increase the volume and value of cross-border shipments of goods (exports and imports) from both the United States and Canada. This expansion, in turn, would be expected to negatively impact the border region's infrastructure and environment through increased traffic congestion and reduced air quality.[22] The agreement would also increase employment in trade-related sectors such as transportation and public utilities, especially in those border communities located on or near the major north-south trade corridors.

3. Impact on the Mexican maquiladora industry and its linkages to the U.S. border region. Due to the rules of origin imposed by NAFTA regarding domestic content provisions required to obtain NAFTA status in terms of low or zero tariff rates for manufactured products, foreign direct investment—from both NAFTA member and nonmember countries—would be increased throughout Mexico, but especially at the border where the larger and most established component of the maquiladora industrial base is found. Such investment would, in turn, stimulate employment in a variety of economic sectors in the U.S. border region.[23]

4. Impact on manufacturing in the border region. Due to reduced tariffs, a more favorable environment for foreign investment in Mexico, and dramatically lower wages in Mexico, manufacturing employment would decline on the U.S. side of the border and rise throughout Mexico, including the border region.

5. Impact on retail sales in the border region. Lower tariffs and liberalized investment laws in Mexico would allow U.S. goods to be sold in Mexico in U.S.–style shopping malls throughout Mexico's northern states, thereby reducing Mexican retail spending in U.S. border communities.

6. Impact on poverty and prosperity in the border region. The overall effect on prosperity, as measured by real income per capita, on the U.S.–Mexican border region would be positive, especially on the Mexican side. That is, the incidence of poverty would fall while prosperity would rise.

The data compiled on the actual demographic and economic situation of the U.S.–Mexican border communities as well as the perceptions of local stakeholders as reported in the surveys will be used to determine the validity of these hypotheses.

A final hypothesis advanced by NOBE/REF researchers relates to those sections of the survey that deal with the perceptions of local stakeholders, especially those associated with governmental or nongovernmental organizations, regarding the need for and access to tools of economic analysis.

7. Need for and access to tools of economic analysis. Given the rapidly changing demographic and economic situation, the surveys were expected to reveal a strong demand for the tools of economic analysis. Furthermore, smaller communities would be less likely than larger ones to actually have access to such tools and Mexican border communities would be less likely than U.S. border communities to have access to such tools.

Findings and Conclusions

What do the findings of this study indicate with respect to these hypotheses? Due to incomplete data sets, especially on the Mexican side, and the limited scope of the research, it is difficult to definitely confirm or reject these hypotheses. However, in general terms, the findings from the data compiled here on border demographic and economic variables, together with findings from other studies and the qualitative surveys, can be regarded as indicative of major trends and suggestive of where clarification through future research is needed.

In analyzing these hypotheses, it must be made clear that the conditions in the border communities are being assessed in the context of a project in process. That is, the NAFTA era has just begun, and its full impact will not be felt for years to come. First, all of the provisions of NAFTA are not yet fully phased in—this will require several more years. In addition, the supposed benefits to Mexico of rising employment, wages, and income, and the reduced pressures to migrate to the United States will take years, perhaps decades, to be realized in a significant way. Meanwhile, a whole host of issues shaping U.S.–Mexican relations and economic integration in the Americas could take unexpected turns that would alter or delay the impact of NAFTA on the region. Mexico itself has many problems—ranging from the Zapatista uprising in Chiapas and the difficult path toward democracy to an economy that has come out of a crisis but has yet to resolve the problems of a weak banking sector. Finally, any scenario must also include many factors on the U.S. side, including the health of the U.S. economy, decisions regarding when and how to implement specific provisions of NAFTA, and U.S. leadership and participation in future economic integration activities in the hemisphere, just to mention a few. With these caveats, the seven hypotheses can be examined.

1. Impact on immigration from the interior of Mexico. While no data on migration were included in this study, it is possible to make some inferences on the basis of what information is available. The expectation was that NAFTA would increase employment, wages, and incomes throughout Mexico, thereby reducing the incentives for internal and international migration from the interior of Mexico.

The data indicate that this has not occurred. Employment, wages, and incomes increased in Mexican border communities, apparently attracting more migration from the interior of the country. Border population growth rates were higher in the NAFTA era (1995–2000) than in the preceding period (1990–1995), while for Mexico as a whole the rate fell substantially (see Table 5). Furthermore, it appears that the improved conditions in Mexican border communities were not enough to offset the incentives drawing people into the United States.

In the U.S. border region the population growth rate did fall during the NAFTA era by approximately 20%, compared to the nation as a whole at about 14%. However, population growth rates during both periods were about twice as high for the border region as for the United States as a whole. This does not mean, however, that international migration from Mexico declined, since there are many factors that enter into such a determination that are outside the scope of this study. The one clear conclusion that can be drawn here is that Mexico's weak national economy in the mid-1990s and the employment opportunities in the rapidly expanding maquiladora sector in the northern border region stimulated significant internal migration.

2. Impact on the border region's infrastructure, environment, and employment in trade-related sectors. As reported above, NAFTA provided for lower tariffs and relaxed investment laws that, in turn, stimulated expanded trade and direct foreign investment in Mexico. Thus, it was logical to expect that border infrastructure and the environment would be negatively impacted during the NAFTA era. The survey data provide some interesting perspectives on this situation.

On the U.S. side, respondents felt that there was a perceptible and strong impact on the region's infrastructure (see Figure 3), yet almost half of the respondents felt that the quality of their county's infrastructure had improved between 1994 and 1999 (see Figure 4). This was apparently due mainly to improved funding made possible by an expanding U.S. economy.

The impact of NAFTA was generally regarded as positive on a wide range of issues, from focusing national attention on border environmental problems to improving cross-border cooperation on environmental problems (see Figure 5). However, there was disagreement on whether the quality of the environment had improved or worsened during the NAFTA era (see Figure 6).

On the Mexican side, the respondents perceived a strong impact on the region's infrastructure due to NAFTA (see Figure 21), but they also felt that the quality of the local infrastructure generally had improved during the NAFTA era (see Figure 22).

As in the United States, most Mexican respondents regarded NAFTA's impact as positive on issues such as focusing national attention on border environmental problems and improving cross-border cooperation on environmental problems (see Figure 23). There was also substantial disagreement on whether the environment had improved, remained the same, or worsened during the 1994–1999 period (see Figure 24). When asked about specific environmental issues, such as air and water quality, there was substantial agreement that these had deteriorated (see Figure 25).

With respect to trade-related employment, a recent study examining the six largest urban subregions of the U.S. border indicates that the transportation and public utilities sector "... has seen not only significant employment growth since the implementation of NAFTA, but increases in its relative importance as well" (Gerber and Rey 1999). Gerber and Rey's study notes that the link between NAFTA and increased employment in this sector may not be causal, but asserts that there is a logical link between increased overland trade and increased employment in this sector.

Also, another study specific to Texas shows that the state has experienced higher transportation employment rates, especially in cities like Laredo. In addition, other direct benefits from international trade have come to the state by way of the federal jobs created in the U.S. Customs Service, the Immigration and Naturalization Service, and other federal law enforcement agencies throughout the Texas-Mexico border region. These jobs are higher paying than the average jobs available in the border cities (Phillips and Manzanares 2001).

3. Impact on the Mexican maquiladora industry and its linkages in the U.S. border region. The data clearly indicate that the maquiladora industry has become an important driver of Mexico's border economy. As noted above, employment in this sector in the border region has more than doubled during the NAFTA era, due mainly to the reduction in Mexican labor costs to foreign investors as a result of the 1994 peso crisis. Another factor that could have influenced non–NAFTA country companies to invest in Mexico is the desire to obtain duty-free access to the North American market. With respect to the growth of linkages between the maquiladora industry and U.S. border urban areas, Hanson (2001) provides evidence that during the 1975–1997 period "the growth of export manufacturing in Mexico can account for a substantial portion of employment growth in U.S. border cities...." The specific sector where employment is created depends on the size of the U.S. city, according to Hanson:

> These findings are consistent with the regional-production-network hypothesis: as U.S. firms move assembly operations to Mexico, they also move complimentary manufacturing activities, such as the production of parts and components, to large U.S. border cities. Hence, border cities appear to specialize in different tasks. Small border cities, such as Nogales and Laredo, are mainly transshipment points in North American trade, while large border cities, such as San Diego and El Paso, are major manufacturing sites (2001, 22).

Another study (Jenner et al. 1998) has similar findings to those of Hanson, but suggests that the quantitative link between Asian maquiladora production in Tijuana and the sourcing of material and service inputs in San Diego (the largest U.S. border city) may be somewhat smaller than what Hanson suggests: only 5% of their inputs are sourced in San Diego with another 8% being purchased from firms in other parts of Southern California. Nevertheless, both of these studies do support the hypothesis that there are cross-border links with the maquiladora industry and as that industry grows those links are likely to grow as well.

4. Impact on manufacturing employment in the border region. Increased cross-border integration implies that manufacturing should move from high- to low-wage areas. In general terms, this was true of U.S. manufacturing plants moving to Mexican border cities. During the 1995–1997 period, manufacturing employment in the Mexican border region grew at an annual rate of 21% compared to just over 2% in the

U.S. border region. However, because suppliers are starting to locate in U.S. border cities, cities like El Paso can still claim the presence of a significant manufacturing sector, a development that can be attributed to the location of the maquiladora sector across the border (Vargas 1998).[24] The high growth rate in Mexico resulted in a significant change in the structure of the labor force. In 1992, only 22.3% of the Mexican border labor force worked in manufacturing, compared to 22% in Mexico as a whole. By 1998, 34.8% of the Mexican border labor force worked in manufacturing, compared to 22.3% for Mexico as a whole.

Gerber and Rey, in their study of six U.S. urban border regions, divide the manufacturing sector into "durables" and "non-durables" and utilizing an analysis of location quotients show that "... the pattern for manufacturing involves a smaller durable goods sector (usually much smaller) and three regions with larger than average non-durable sector" (1999, 12) Thus, during the NAFTA era, some cities suffered a loss of manufacturing jobs, while others experienced slight gains. The case of El Paso is an interesting example in terms of what has happened to different manufacturing sectors. There, losses in the apparel sector have been offset by gains by plants that supply plastic-injection molding to the maquiladoras. In spite of this, manufacturing employment has not registered positive gains because the losses in apparel, a more labor-intensive sector, are larger than the gains in plastic-injection molding, a more capital-intensive sector that requires much less labor, although the labor component is highly skilled and better compensated (Vargas 1998).

5. Impact on retail sales in the border region. Again, the logical pattern here suggests that increased integration would imply losses of retail sales on the U.S. side and gains on the Mexican side. The data, gathered from a variety of sources, tend to support this hypothesis, with some modification.

The data on border transactions indicate that Mexicans have been buying less in the United States and more in Mexico during the NAFTA era and Gerber and Rey (1999) shows that location quotients in retail trade, while significantly larger than in the national economy, have declined in importance during the same period. The shift-share analysis presented earlier indicates that retail trade grew in absolute numbers during the NAFTA era, but apparently at a slower rate, resulting in a decline in the relative importance of that sector compared to previous periods. However, even though Mexicans are buying less from U.S. stores due primarily to the availability of the same goods in Mexico, Mexican purchases in the U.S border region are still substantial. For instance, in El Paso 30 to 40% of retail sales are attributed to Mexicans. More importantly, in the El Paso downtown area, Mexicans represent up to 90% of any given store's sales.

6. *Impact on poverty and prosperity in the border region.* There are several indicators that can be utilized to determine what has occurred with respect to per capita income. However, data availablity differs in the United States and Mexico.

On the U.S. side (see Tables 3 and 4), measures of poverty for the U.S. border region during the NAFTA era were not available. However, Peach (1997), using census data from 1969, 1979, and 1989, determined that not only was income inequality in the region greater than in the nation, but that all common measures of income distribution indicate a general trend toward greater inequality during the 1980s. Although there are many determinants of poverty, these data—together with the general trend toward increased income inequality in the United States—suggest that the incidence of poverty in the region, especially in the Texas border region, rose during the 1990s. Another indicator of the high degree of poverty is the low percentage of the population 25 years old or older with a high school diploma.

With respect to prosperity, the data on the average annual percent change in per capita income in Table 4 show two important trends. First, while income increased at an annual rate of 2.7% during the 1994–1997 period, the rate of increase was lower than in the previous period from 1990 to 1993. Second, during the 1990–1993 period, per capita income in the border region increased at a higher rate than the United States as a whole, while in the 1994–1997 period, the rate of increase in the border region was less than that of the United States as a whole.

This means that during the period after the implementation of NAFTA—a period of vigorous expansion in the U.S. economy—the border region underperformed the nation as a whole. Therefore, while income per capita rose throughout the 1990s, the income gap between the border region and the nation fell during the 1990–1993 period.

During the 1994–1997 period, after the implementation of NAFTA, that gap increased.

The comparison of U.S. border performance in the 1990s with that of the overall national economy, however, is perhaps unfair and would be expected to yield skewed results showing an underperforming border region. A more appropriate comparison would be between the U.S. border and other similar subregions of the United States. For example, a study comparing the Texas border with areas having similar characteristics, such as Kentucky, West Virginia, or Mississippi, showed that the Texas border outperformed these regions in the United States in job growth as well as earnings per job during the 1990s (Phillips and Dittmar 1999). Although the poor counties along the Texas border did underperform these same regions during the 1990s in per capita income, it should be noted that Texas border counties have larger households than the rest of the United States, which tends to bias the per capita income figures downward.[25]

On the Mexican side (see Table 5), with respect to poverty, the data for the Mexican border region are clear. The percentage of the work force in the border region earning less than the minimum wage declined during the 1990s. In Mexico as a whole, however, that percentage increased significantly, increasing from 8.5% during the 1990–1994 period to 11.2% during the 1994–1998 period.

From 1990 to 2000, per capita GDP (in constant 1993 pesos) at the border increased from $15,350 to $19,580—an increase of almost 28%. In Mexico as a whole, the increase was only 3%. This difference must be adjusted to account for the impact of the higher inflation rate normally experienced in the Mexican border region. Inflation along the border is generally estimated to be about 25% higher than the rest of Mexico.[26] However, even accounting for 25% higher inflation, real per capita GDP can be estimated to have risen by 21%, compared to 3% in Mexico overall. The border population, therefore, seems to have enjoyed a significantly greater improvement in purchasing power than people in the rest of Mexico.

In light of information presented in this study, some important contrasts can be seen in the changing patterns of poverty and prosperity when comparing U.S. and Mexican border communities during the NAFTA era. First, the border areas of both countries are experiencing rapid population growth—growth at a faster rate than in each nation as a whole—and it is clear that there is a shift of population to the border region. Second, economic activity is accelerating on both sides of the border at higher rates than in the respective national economies. However, in U.S. border communities the most jobs are being created in the service sector. In contrast, it is mainly the maquiladora assembly-manufacturing sector that is driving job and income growth on the Mexican side. Third, Mexican border communities experienced a surge in economic activity—not due solely to NAFTA—that has produced average incomes exceeding those in the rest of Mexico. In contrast, the relatively rapid growth of employment in U.S. border communities has failed to boost prosperity at a rate commensurate with the rest of the United States.

Fourth, in the U.S. border region, economic and population growth are taking place as growth of per capita income lags behind that of the United States as a whole.[27] Thus, the gap between the average income of U.S. border residents and the average income of the general U.S. population is widening. Additionally, despite significant growth in the number of jobs in U.S. border communities, unemployment remains high and wages remain low compared to the rest of the United States.[28] In contrast, in the Mexican border region, economic growth is taking place while growth of per capita income outstrips that of Mexico as a whole. Also, in contrast to the U.S. border, the Mexican border region has experienced lower unemployment and higher wages compared to the rest of Mexico. Of course, wages are still significantly lower than those paid on the U.S. side of the border. If Mexican border per capita income continues to rise at a more rapid rate than the rate on the U.S. side, the two wage levels would eventually converge. More research is needed to determine the exact behavior of wages in both the U.S. and Mexican border regions.

7. Need for and access to tools of economic analysis. Findings regarding the perceived need for and access to tools of analysis in both U.S. and Mexican border communities are summarized in Table 18.

The following observations based on Table 18 are relevant to the hypothesis:

- In general, there is a much greater perceived need for analytical tools in the U.S. border region than in the Mexican border region, as determined by adding the responses of "very important" and "somewhat important" and by the percentage of respondents answering this section (65% in Mexico and 95% in

Table 18. U.S.–Mexican Border Communities Access to Tools of Analysis

Type of System	Importance (Very or Somewhat)	With Access	Regular Use
U.S. Border Communities			
Demographic Modeling	83%	55%	75%
Economic Modeling	79%	37%	58%
Economic Monitoring	78%	44%	75%
Environmental Monitoring	61%	27%	66%
Infrastructure Needs Forecasting	81%	37%	80%
Quality-of-Life Monitoring	76%	23%	77%
Mexican Border Communities			
Demographic	93%	29%	60%
Economic Modeling	94%	21%	49%
Economic Monitoring	97%	37%	66%
Environmental Monitoring	87%	23%	65%
Infrastructure Needs Forecasting	98%	26%	67%
Quality-of-Life Monitoring	93%	18%	67%

the United States). On the U.S. side, the most important analytical tools are demographic modeling systems and systems for forecasting infrastructure needs, while the least important are systems for monitoring quality of life and the environment.

- On the Mexican side, the most important analytical tools indicated by survey participants are systems for monitoring the economy and for forecasting infrastructure needs, while the least important are systems for monitoring the environment.
- The differences in terms of strength of demand and utilization rates are much higher in the United States than in Mexico. However, it is noteworthy that systems for monitoring the environment were perceived as being least needed on both sides.
- Analysis of the data also revealed that larger communities on both sides of the border have much greater access to these analytical tools and that U.S. communities have much greater access than Mexican communities.

Implications of the Study for Public Policy and Further Research

In introducing this final section, it is important to observe once again that the U.S.–Mexican border region is not a homogeneous region.

Variations with respect to demographic and economic size and structure as well as geographic characteristics are very large and undoubtedly contribute to the differences in economic performance that this study has identified. Of course, all of these communities are conditioned by one important and unique feature: their proximity to the international boundary brings economic, social, administrative, and ecological linkages with their cross-border neighbors. For many communities, such proximity also implies a role as an international entrepôt, a corridor for the transshipment of goods and services. It is this feature that differentiates them from other communities within their respective countries and creates a cross-border interdependence that transcends national jurisdictions. Thus, when public policy makers look at the issues facing their own communities, it is essential that they view them within an international and cross-border context.

It is also important for policy makers to view the border situation in a dynamic context. For over fifty years, population growth in the border region's urban areas has been high by national standards. Projections of border region population to the year 2020 reflect these historically high growth rates and exhibit considerable variation (Peach and Williams 2000). These projections imply a combined population of the 25 U.S. border counties and 38 border municipios ranging from 15.1 million to 24 million by the year 2020. The first figure assumes no new migration into the region and the last assumes that migration will continue at 1995 levels. Thus, the likely total border population in 2020 will be well over 20 million. In 1995, the base year data for these projections, the border region population was approximately 10.6 million persons (Peach and Williams 2000). Given the probability of high demographic growth, the problems of today will be magnified in 10 to 20 years in the absence of informed, collaborative, cross-border public policy.

This study has revealed and confirmed the existence of a number of issues that need to be addressed if U.S.–Mexican border communities are to achieve their economic and quality-of-life potential. Perhaps the most significant implications of the study can be derived from the concluding paragraph under the sixth hypothesis, "Impact on poverty and prosperity in the border region."

In the U.S. border region, economic and population growth is taking place as growth of per capita income lags behind that of the United States as a whole. Thus, with the exception of San Diego County, the gap between the average incomes of U.S. border residents and the average income of the general U.S. population is widening. Additionally, despite significant growth in the number of jobs in U.S. border communities, unemployment remains high and wages remain low compared to the rest of the United States. In contrast, in the Mexican border region economic growth is taking place as growth of per capita income outstrips that of Mexico as a whole. Also, in contrast to the U.S. border, the Mexican border region has experienced lower unemployment and higher wages compared to the rest of Mexico.

Migration, Prosperity, and Poverty Issues

This conclusion implies both good news and bad news regarding Mexican immigration into the border regions of the United States. The good news is that as this convergence of wages continues, the supply push motivating Mexican migration will likely diminish. That is, even though the convergence of wages is downward in relation to U.S. wages, the potential Mexican immigrant apparently still sees the wage differential as significant enough to move across the border. But since there is convergence, at some point the difference will narrow to the point that it is no longer a sufficient incentive and the migrant flow will normalize to levels similar to those from countries with compensation levels comparable to the United States. The bad news is that the current conditions imply that it will take decades, if not generations, to dissipate the supply pressure. More research is needed, but it certainly appears that in the period studied here the supply pressure has not abated. More work is needed to integrate the empirical and theoretical research on immigration being done at the national level with the analysis of specific demographic and economic structures and performance of the U.S. border region as represented by this study.

Another important issue related to immigration is the alleged need of U.S. agricultural firms to import workers on a temporary basis. U.S. employers are anxious to hire Mexican immigrants and immigrants from other lower-wage countries. For example, recent research on the economy of the Yuma, Arizona, area documented an intense lobbying effort by local agribusiness leaders to pass a guest worker bill in the U.S. Congress that would facilitate a much larger flow of agricultural workers from Mexico (Schmaedick 2001). This effort is not confined solely to Yuma. In fact, Yuma leaders joined the Western

Growers Association in this effort in Washington, D.C. The association represents agricultural interests in all the states along the Mexican border. Recognition of the convergence of wages should be part of this debate. Since it is a vital factor in such a discussion, much more research should be undertaken to determine the magnitude, speed, and forces driving it.

An even larger issue is the question of the growing gap between the average income of U.S. border residents and the average income of the general U.S. population. This is a palpably negative phenomenon observable over the NAFTA era. While the alleged benefits to the nation as a whole are widely touted, the implications of the growing wage gap call out for policies to address it. The implications are very broad because "in spite of significant growth in the number of jobs in U.S. border communities, unemployment remains high...." As the study indicates, an analogous situation is occurring in Mexico, where the north benefits while the rest of Mexico lags behind. Both countries are faced with the challenging task of seeking policies to mobilize benefits to those who are not currently participating in the economic benefits of NAFTA, or even worse, suffering in deteriorating conditions because of economic liberalization.

While there is a strong temptation to try to analyse why these changes occurred, it is important to remember that this study was not designed to identify or quantify the effects of NAFTA or other factors on the border economy. As pointed out in the introduction, the study was designed to determine what kinds of changes occurred during the NAFTA era. Defining causality for such changes was simply beyond the scope of the present project. Recent studies on the Texas border economy, which do venture into such territory, indicate that there are many factors influencing employment growth and income levels there. These include population growth, migration, and education, as well as infrastructure policies and growth of the Mexican maquiladora industry.[29] It is the hope of NOBE/REF researchers that unanswered questions raised by this study can be addressed in a systematic way by future efforts.

Maquiladora Issues

There are still many important issues surrounding the role of the maquiladoras in national and regional development, even after more than 35 years of operation. Many of these issues are raised by this study and deserve further research and attention in the policy-making arena. To what extent has the development of the maquiladora sector been responsible for the phenomenal economic growth of the Mexican border region? Proponents tend to say it has been the single most important driving force, if not the only driving force, of the border economy and that the maquiladora sector has been a major force in stimulating the Mexican economy during the 1990s. To support this position, they point to evidence that wages paid in the maquiladora sector have grown at a faster rate than the rest of Mexican industry and the maquiladora industry has been a powerful force in Mexico's regional and technological development. Opponents generally criticize the maquiladora industry by saying that it is an enclave sector with few linkages to the national or regional economy of Mexico, does not contribute to national or regional development, and deliberately suppresses wages. Given these two opposing viewpoints, it is obvious that additional research should explore these and the following issues:

- What impact have the maquiladoras made on real wage levels in Mexico as a whole and specifically in the border region? What effect has the demand for labor created by the maquiladoras had on real incomes? Has the wage effect, whatever it has been, impacted only the communities immediately affected by the presence of the maquiladoras or has there been a general upward or downward pressure on wages throughout the country?
- What has the maquiladora sector's net impact been on the environment and environmental policy and enforcement in Mexico? Has the liberalization of the Mexican economy and its integration into the global economy accelerated the adoption and enforcement of stricter environmental laws and regulations that cite maquiladoras as models in environmental compliance? Or, have the maquiladoras used their significant economic clout to force compromises and keep policies lax or even erode them? Everyone has an opinion, but what are the facts? This is an area where much needed research would provide valuable input to the policy-making process.
- What have maquiladoras contributed to the evolution of Mexican industry? Has the touted phenomenon of technology transfer actually occurred and, if so, how has it benefited the devel-

opment of the border region? Have benefits been isolated in the export sector with no spin-off benefits to domestic industry? Has the workforce experienced an increase in essential competencies and capabilities? Again, everyone has an opinion and there has been some good work done in this area, but there is still room for more evidence to resolve the debate.

In general, there is a need to structure the evaluation of the maquiladora sector in terms of a broader cost-benefit context that would seek to identify the net benefits or costs of this sector to the larger economy of the border communities in order to determine how this sector can more positively contribute to both the quality of life and the economic development of the region. The maquiladora sector has, after all, become the *de facto* focal point of the border economy and, especially since 1994, has been recognized as the major driving force of the national economy. For the border communities, it is very important to examine the linkages, both positive and negative, between the maquiladoras and the domestic nonexport sector of the economy. Such an analysis should examine whether the externalities that have benefited the maquiladora sector may have impeded or even damaged the performance of the domestic-oriented economy of the border communities. Or, if positive externalities generated by the industry—such as the creation of human capital for the country through the ongoing training of its workforce—benefited the larger Mexican economy.

Issues Regarding Cross-Border Transactions

The conclusions reached in this study regarding retail sales (hypothesis 5) suggest that Mexicans are buying less in the United States and more in Mexico as the impact of liberalization and NAFTA takes hold in communities along the border. This is an extremely important finding for U.S. border communities. Should they encourage the continued development of a retail sector that requires growing sales to Mexicans to remain viable? For example, in Yuma, Arizona, Kmart, Walmart, and Home Depot all have been encouraged to build stores larger than the local consumer base can support on the assumption that the demand from Mexico will make them profitable. More research is needed to determine the magnitude and rate of the shift by the Mexican consumer to Mexican retail outlets. This will inform local policy makers in U.S. border communities and guide their decisions regarding incentives and encouragement provided to retail developers. In general, employment trends among the sectors deserve more attention for the same reason. Therefore, the work presented on shift-share analysis should be extended and amplified. The results of this work need to be communicated to local economic development organizations and others responsible for formulating local development policy.

Issues Regarding Tools of Economic Analysis

The conclusions of this study regarding the communities' need for and access to tools for environmental, infrastructure, and economic analysis are somewhat disturbing for several reasons. While the recognition of the importance of these tools is reasonably high among the U.S. respondents (80%) and generally supported by about 60% of Mexican respondents, the higher these rates are, the higher is the awareness that sound public policy decision making requires information and analysis. Thus, it is a matter of concern that the response to environmental monitoring was important to only 60% of the respondents on both sides of the border, indicating a relatively low level of environmental concern by leaders in border communities.

Although anticipated, it is nonetheless disturbing that such a low percentage of communities have access to these analytical tools. This is especially true in the smaller U.S. communities and in Mexican communities where, historically, local government has not been a major player in the determination of regional economic development policy. This strongly indicates the need for a policy of cost sharing to assist the communities that desire these tools for monitoring and analyzing their local situation but are unable to cover the full cost of setting up and maintaining them. There also seems to be a need for a program to orient and train local planning and development employees, as well as the general public, as to the value of these tools.

A Strategy for Following Up This Study's Findings

While these are only a sampling of the issues that arise from the study's findings, it is suggested that any efforts to address these issues through organized research be done in collaboration with local stakeholders and state and national agencies on both sides of the border. Specifically, the following two-step strategy is suggested:

First, NOBE/REF researchers—perhaps in collaboration with other organizations—should convene "focus group" meetings in each border community made up of the respondents to the surveys of the present study and others. Such meetings would be used to detail the unique problems of each of the communities and to determine what they could actually use in terms of indicators and analytical tools in order to both monitor their own situations and draw attention to the special needs of border communities in their respective political capitals. This step should require approximately six months.

Second, the NOBE/REF researchers, together with local stakeholders, should prepare a larger research design based on the information gathered in the focus groups and in this study in order to launch a project that would achieve the following:

- Analyze the key prosperity/economic, environmental infrastructure, and quality-of-life issues generated by this study and the focus groups
- Create indicators and analytical tools that could be used by border communities on an on-going basis
- Maintain liaisons among local stakeholders, governmental agencies, and NOBE/REF researchers through workshops and periodic conferences. This phase will require 18 to 24 months

This study was intended as an initial and preliminary effort, identifying what is known and what is not known about the U.S.–Mexican border region. Therefore, it follows that the most important conclusion of this study is precisely that much more needs to be done in terms of analyzing and understanding the region in a systematic fashion.

Notes

Chapter 1: Introduction

1. Negotiations on NAFTA began in 1991 and all three countries, Canada, Mexico, and the United States, approved the agreement in 1993. During this period, businesses began preparations on how to best take advantage of the new business environment that they expected to be established upon implementation in January 1994, which included lower tariff and nontariff barriers as well as liberalized foreign investment laws in Mexico.
2. Economic indicators could include price indices and unemployment rates as well as various measures of production, sales, consumption, and banking activity. Quality-of-life indicators could include measures of poverty, literacy and educational attainment, housing, health, and sanitation.

Chapter 2: U.S.–Mexican Border Communities: An Overview

3. For more details on this period see Oscar J. Martínez, ed., *U.S.–Mexico Borderlands: Historical and Contemporary Perspectives* (Wilmington: Scholarly Resources, 1996).
4. Economists refer to this phenomenon as "border transactions." These mainly consist of purchases and sales of products that are not reported as imports or exports nor processed and recorded by customs.
5. Inflation in the United States between 1954 and 1976 was 112%, while in Mexico it was 279%.
6. Mexico's debt crisis of the early 1980s was the decisive event in opening up the Mexican economy from Import Substitution Industrialization (1950s–1970s) to Export Oriented Industrialization (1980s–present). Most of the market-oriented reforms and efforts toward trade liberalization that now characterize Mexico's economy have occurred since the early 1980s. In the period of

import substitution, government participation in the economy and protective tariffs were quite high. Mexico only joined the General Agreement on Tariffs and Trade (GATT) in 1986.

7. According to a recent study "the growth of export manufacturing in Mexico can account for a substantial portion of employment growth in U.S. border cities over the same period (1975–1997)" (Hanson 2001).
8. For a recent update on the maquiladora industry see Lucinda Vargas, "Maquiladoras 2000: Still Growing," *Business Frontier* 3 (2000). Available at <http://www.dallasfed.org/htm/pubs/pdfs/busfront/300.pdf>. For a brief overview of the maquiladora industry under NAFTA see James Gerber, "Whither the Maquiladora? A Look at the Growth Prospects for the Industry after 2001," San Diego Dialogue working paper #E-99-1, University of California at San Diego, La Jolla, Calif., 1999.
9. Las Cruces, New Mexico, a city of approximately 75,000 inhabitants, is located some 75 miles from the border and northwest of El Paso, Texas. Therefore, much of the cross-border retail trade from the Mexican state of Chihuahua has traditionally gone to El Paso, not Las Cruces.
10. San Ysidro is the largest border crossing point in the San Diego–Tijuana area for noncommercial vehicles and pedestrians.
11. Measured as multiples of minimum wages.
12. Altos Hornos de México, a steel mill and the largest single employer of the state, has been in crisis since 1985.

Chapter 3: Changing Demographic and Economic Patterns in the U.S.–Mexican Border Region during the NAFTA Era

13. While many studies have attempted to assess the overall impact of NAFTA at the national level, only a few have attempted to assess its impact on the border region (see Patrick 1996, and Peach 2000).
14. Perhaps a comparison of the border with the nation as a whole is unfair since a more appropriate comparison might be one that looks at the border's performance in relation to other similar subregions within the country. This comparison is made in Keith Phillips, "Border Region Makes Progress in the 1990s," *Vista*

December 1999. Available at <http://www.dallasfed.org/htm/pubs/pdfs/vista/dec_99.pdf>. Indeed, when the border is compared with other similar subregions in the country in the 1990s the border comes out as a better performer than these other areas.

15. According to calculations based on Census Bureau estimates as presented in Peach and Adkisson (2000), despite historically high in-migration rates, two-thirds of the border region's population change between 1990 and 1998 can be attributed to natural increase.
16. The conclusion of Gruben and Kiser (2001) is that NAFTA has not been a determinant of maquiladora industry growth. Rather, the three factors found to impact growth in the industry are U.S. industrial production and Mexican-to-U.S. and Mexican-to-Asian manufacturing wage ratios.
17. Banco de México, which generates these data, lumps all cross-border trade of merchandise and services, such as tourism, together as represented by the exchange of Mexican for American money and vice versa. This is determined by estimating the volume of trade dealt with by banks in Mexican and U.S. currency and checks under $100.
18. In December 1994, the Mexican peso crisis dramatically changed the dollar-peso relationship, increasing the border's surplus.
19. This coefficient indicates the percentage retained by Mexico of every dollar that comes into the Mexican border region.
20. An extensive program was begun in 1988 to promote and facilitate the construction of shopping centers along the border. Among the conditions that must be fulfilled by businessmen receiving permits for the establishment of shopping centers were the following: (1) the company's capital must be underwritten by Mexicans or, in exceptional instances, by a Mexican majority through the issue of registered stock; (2) the imported products must be sold at prices comparable to those charged for the same items in the United States; and (3) at least 50% of the sales must be of domestic products.

Chapter 5: Conclusions and Recommendations

21. For a mainstream discussion and critique of the agreement itself see Hufbauer and Schott 1993.

22. For this reason, the NAFTA side agreements on the environment provided for two new institutions, the North American Development Bank (NADB) and the Border Environment Cooperation Commission (BECC).
23. However, in 2001, Mexico instituted the Programas de Promoción Sectoral or PROSEC (Sectoral Promotion Programs), which allow preferential duty treatment of certain inputs of non–NAFTA origin.
24. See Lucinda Vargas, "El Paso's Labor-Mismatch Dilemma," *Business Frontier* 1 (1998). Federal Reserve Bank of Dallas, El Paso Branch.
25. Tom Fullerton has made this observation in analyzing per capita income conditions at the border. See "El Paso Incomes Hit Record Low," *The El Paso Times*, 4 May 2001.
26. See estimate developed for Tijuana in Bernardo Gonzáles Aréchiga and Noé Arón Fuentes, "¿Es Tijuana realmente una ciudad cara?" *Ciclos, Revista del Noroeste*, Año 3 (28) 1988.
27. In per capita income analysis, the size of a household does matter and border cities have larger households than the rest of the nation (Fullerton 2001).
28. It is important, once again, to keep in mind that a more appropriate comparison of border performance might be with similar regions in the United States rather than with the nation as a whole. This more relevant comparison is made in Keith Phillips, "Border Region Makes Progress in the 1990s," *Vista* December 1999. Available at <http://www.dallasfed.org/htm/pubs/pdfs/vista/dec_99.pdf>.
29. See *The Border Economy* June 2001. Available at <http://www.dallasfed.org/htm/pubs/border /tbe_6_01.pdf>.

References

Banco de Informacion Sectorial (BIS). 2001. *Establecimientos y empleo.* Accessed February 7 and 12, 2001. Available at <http://www.spice.gob.mx/ siem2000/bis>.

Banco de México. 2001. *Informe annual, 2000.* Mexico: Banco de México.

Clement, Norris C., Gustavo del Castillo Vera, James Gerber, William A. Kerr, Alan J. MacFadyen, Stanford Shedd, Eduardo Zepeda, and Diana Alarcón. 1999. *North American economic integration: Theory and practice.* Northhampton, Mass.: Edward Elgar Publishing, Inc.

Economic Policy Institute. 2001. *NAFTA at seven: Its impact on workers in all three nations.* Briefing Paper. Washington, D.C. Available at <http://www.epinet.org/briefingpapers/nafta01/nafta-at-7.pdf>.

Gerber, James. 1999. Whither the maquiladora? A look at the growth prospects for the industry after 2001. San Diego Dialogue working paper #E-99-1. La Jolla: University of California at San Diego.

Gerber, James, and Serge Rey. 1999. The employment dynamics of regional economies on the U.S.–Mexican border (unpublished manuscript).

Gruben, William C., and Sherry L. Kiser. 2001. NAFTA and maquiladoras: Is the growth connected? In *The Border Economy.* Dallas: Federal Reserve Bank of Dallas. Available at <http://www.dallasfed.org/htm/pubs/border/tbe_gruben.pdf>.

Hanson, Gordon H. 2001. U.S.–Mexico integration and regional economies: Evidence from border-city pairs. *Journal of Urban Economics* 50 (2): 259–87.

Hufbauer, Gary Clyde, and Jeffrey J. Schott. 1993. *NAFTA: An assessment.* Washington, D.C.: Institute for International Economics.

Instituto Nacional de Estadistica, Geografía e Informática (INEGI). 1991. *XII censo industrial, 1986: Datos municipales, referentes a 1985.* 4 vols. Aguascalientes, Ags.: El Instituto.

Instituto Nacional de Estadistica, Geografía e Informática (INEGI). 1992. *XIII censo industrial, 1989: Resultados definitivos.* 32 vols. Aguascalientes, Ags.: El Instituto.

Instituto Nacional de Estadistica, Geografía e Informática (INEGI). 1992. *XIII censo industrial, 1989: Resultados definitivos*. 32 vols. Aguascalientes, Ags.: El Instituto.

Instituto Nacional de Estadistica, Geografía e Informática (INEGI). 1994. *Sistema automatizado de información censal (SAIC 3.1): Censo económicos*. Disco Compacto. Aguascalientes, Ags.: El Instituto.

Jenner, Stephen, Wim Douw, and Boudewijn Koops. 1998. Sourcing strategies of Asian manufacturers and the development of local linkages in San Diego and Tijuana. *Journal of Borderlands Studies* 13 (2): 19–48.

Patrick, J. Michael. 1996. A preliminary assessment of NAFTA's impact on the Texas border economy. *Journal of Borderlands Studies* 11 (2) 23–50.

Peach, James T., and Richard V. Adkisson. 2000. NAFTA and economic activity along the U.S.–Mexico border. *Journal of Economic Issues* 34 (2): 481–89.

Peach, James T., and James Williams. 2000. Population and economic dynamics on the U.S.–Mexican border: Past, present and future. In *The U.S.–Mexican border environment: A road map to a sustainable 2020*, edited by Paul Ganster. San Diego: San Diego State University Press.

Phillips, Keith, and Eric Dittmar. 1999. Border region makes progress in the 1990s. *Vista* December 1999. Available at <http://www.dallasfed.org/htm/pubs/pdfs/vista/dec_99.pdf>.

Phillips, Keith, and Carlos Manzanares. 2001. Transportation infrastructure and the border economy. In *The Border Economy*. Available at <http://www.dallasfed.org/htm/pubs/border/tbe_phillips.pdf>.

Rey, Serge, Paul Ganster, Gustavo del Castillo, Juan Alvarez, Ken Shellhammer, Norris Clement, and Alan Sweedler. 1998. The San Diego–Tijuana region. In *Integrating cities and regions: North America faces globalization*, edited by James W. Wilkie and Clint E. Smith. Guadalajara: Universidad de Guadalajara.

Salas, Carlos. 2001. The impact of NAFTA on wages and incomes in Mexico. In *NAFTA at seven: Its impact on workers in all three nations*. Economic Policy Institute Briefing Paper. Washington, D.C. Available at <http://www.epinet.org/briefingpapers/nafta01/nafta-at-7.pdf>.

Schmaedick, Gerald L. 2001. Integration of cross-border communities: The case of San Luis Rio Colorado, Sonora and Yuma County, Arizona. Paper presented at the annual meeting of the Association for Borderlands Studies, 20 April 2001 at Reno, Nevada.

Texas Center for Border Economic and Enterprise Development (TCBEED). 2001. *Border trade data.* Available at <http://www.tamiu.edu/coba/bti>.

U.S. Department of Commerce. n.d. Regional economic information system: 1966–1999. CD-ROM. Washington, D.C.: The Bureau.

Vargas, Lucinda. 1998. El Paso's labor-mismatch dilemma. *Business Frontier* 1 (1998). Federal Reserve Bank of Dallas, El Paso Branch.

Vargas, Lucinda. 2000a. NAFTA's first five years (part 2). *Business Frontier* 1 (2000). Available at <http://www.dallasfed.org/htm/pubs/pdfs/busfront/100.pdf>.

Vargas, Lucinda. 2000b. Maquiladoras 2000: Still growing. *Business Frontier* 3 (2000). Available at <http://www.dallasfed.org/htm/pubs/pdfs/busfront/300.pdf>.

Index